W9-BRX-458

Saved by an Angel

ALSO BY DOREEN VIRTUE

Books/Kits/Oracle Board

The Angel Therapy® Handbook
Angel Words (with Grant Virtue)
Archangels 101
The Healing Miracles of Archangel Raphael
The Art of Raw Living Food (with Jenny Ross)
Signs from Above (with Charles Virtue)
The Miracles of Archangel Michael
Angel Numbers 101
Solomon's Angels (a novel)
My Guardian Angel (with Amy Oscar)
Angel Blessings Candle Kit (with Grant Virtue; includes booklet, CD, journal, etc.)
Thank You, Angels! (children's book with Kristina Tracy)
Healing Words from the Angels
How to Hear Your Angels
Realms of the Earth Angels
Fairies 101
Daily Guidance from Your Angels
Divine Magic
How to Give an Angel Card Reading Kit
Angels 101
Angel Guidance Board
Goddesses & Angels
Crystal Therapy (with Judith Lukomski)
Connecting with Your Angels Kit (includes booklet, CD, journal, etc.)
Angel Medicine
The Crystal Children
Archangels & Ascended Masters
Earth Angels
Messages from Your Angels
Angel Visions II
Eating in the Light (with Becky Prelitz, M.F.T., R.D.)
The Care and Feeding of Indigo Children
Healing with the Fairies
Angel Visions
Divine Prescriptions
Healing with the Angels
"I'd Change My Life If I Had More Time"
Divine Guidance
Chakra Clearing
Angel Therapy®
The Lightworker's Way
Constant Craving A–Z
Constant Craving
The Yo-Yo Diet Syndrome
Losing Your Pounds of Pain

Audio/CD Programs

Angel Therapy® Meditations
Archangels 101 (abridged audio book)
Fairies 101 (abridged audio book)
Goddesses & Angels (abridged audio book)
Angel Medicine (available as both 1- and 2-CD sets)
Angels among Us (with Michael Toms)
Messages from Your Angels (abridged audio book)
Past-Life Regression with the Angels
Divine Prescriptions
The Romance Angels
Connecting with Your Angels
Manifesting with the Angels
Karma Releasing
Healing Your Appetite, Healing Your Life
Healing with the Angels
Divine Guidance
Chakra Clearing

DVD Program

How to Give an Angel Card Reading

Oracle Cards (44 or 45 divination cards and guidebook)

Romance Angels Oracle Cards (available February 2012)
Life Purpose Oracle Cards (available August 2011)
Archangel Raphael Healing Oracle Cards
Archangel Michael Oracle Cards
Angel Therapy® Oracle Cards
Magical Messages from the Fairies Oracle Cards
Ascended Masters Oracle Cards
Daily Guidance from Your Angels Oracle Cards
Saints & Angels Oracle Cards
Magical Unicorns Oracle Cards
Goddess Guidance Oracle Cards
Archangel Oracle Cards
Magical Mermaids and Dolphins Oracle Cards
Messages from Your Angels Oracle Cards
Healing with the Fairies Oracle Cards
Healing with the Angels Oracle Cards

All of the above are available at your local bookstore, or may be ordered by visiting: Hay House USA: **www.hayhouse.com®**; Hay House Australia: **www.hayhouse.com.au**; Hay House UK: **www.hayhouse.co.uk**; Hay House South Africa: **www.hayhouse.co.za**; Hay House India: **www.hayhouseco.in**

Doreen's website: **www.AngelTherapy.com**

Saved by an Angel

True Accounts of People Who Have Had
Extraordinary Experiences with Angels . . .
and How YOU Can, Too!

DOREEN VIRTUE

HAY HOUSE, INC.
Carlsbad, California • New York City
London • Sydney • Johannesburg
Vancouver • Hong Kong • New Delhi

Copyright © 2011 by Doreen Virtue

Published and distributed in the United States by: Hay House, Inc.: www.hay house.com • *Published and distributed in Australia by:* Hay House Australia Pty. Ltd.: www.hayhouse.com.au • *Published and distributed in the United Kingdom by:* Hay House UK, Ltd.: www.hayhouse.co.uk • *Published and distributed in the Republic of South Africa by:* Hay House SA (Pty), Ltd.: www.hayhouse.co.za • *Distributed in Canada by:* Raincoast: www.raincoast.com • *Published in India by:* Hay House Publishers India: www.hayhouse.co.in

Editorial supervision: Jill Kramer • *Project editor:* Alex Freemon
Cover design: Steve Williams • *Interior design:* Jenny Richards

All rights reserved. No part of this book may be reproduced by any mechanical, photographic, or electronic process, or in the form of a phonographic recording; nor may it be stored in a retrieval system, transmitted, or otherwise be copied for public or private use—other than for "fair use" as brief quotations embodied in articles and reviews—without prior written permission of the publisher.

The author of this book does not dispense medical advice or prescribe the use of any technique as a form of treatment for physical, emotional, or medical problems without the advice of a physician, either directly or indirectly. The intent of the author is only to offer information of a general nature to help you in your quest for emotional and spiritual well-being. In the event you use any of the information in this book for yourself, which is your constitutional right, the author and the publisher assume no responsibility for your actions.

Portions of this book were published in *Angel Visions* (Hay House, 2000) and *Angel Visions II* (Hay House, 2001) by Doreen Virtue.

Library of Congress Cataloging-in-Publication Data

Saved by an angel : true accounts of people who have had extraordinary experiences with angels--and how you can, too! / [compiled by] Doreen Virtue. -- 1st ed.
      p. cm.
   ISBN 978-1-4019-3361-6 (tradepaper : alk. paper) -- ISBN 978-1-4019-3362-3 (digital) 1. Angels--Miscellanea. 2. Spiritualism. 3. Visions. I. Virtue, Doreen, 1958-
   BF1999.S3422 2011
   202'.15--dc22

                                 2010052699

Tradepaper ISBN: 978-1-4019-3361-6
Digital ISBN: 978-1-4019-3362-3

14 13 12 11   4 3 2 1
1st edition, June 2011

Printed in the United States of America

Thank You, God,
for sending angels to
protect, guide, and love us all.

Contents

Preface

Have you had an angel experience? Ever since my life was saved by an angel during an armed carjacking in 1995, I've devoted my time to researching and teaching these experiences. Just within the past five years, it seems that an increasing number of us have seen, heard, or felt the presence of a celestial being, based on the ever-growing number of angel stories I've received.

Fifty-five percent of the 1,700 American adults surveyed by Baylor University in 2008 reported that they had been "protected from harm by a guardian angel." The survey included a statistically significant number of people who didn't consider themselves religious, which illustrates how angels help everyone equally.

The angels are here among us right now, and *your* guardian angels are with you as you read this sentence. They're making their presence known in order to help calm earthly fears about the future and to guide you to the path of your Divine life purpose.

This book contains true accounts of people whose lives have been saved or changed by angelic intervention. Some of these stories are favorites culled from my previous books *Angel Visions* and *Angel Visions II*. As you'll read, the people involved are ordinary folks. You don't need to be a saint or lead a perfect life in order to connect with angels. Every person has guardian angels who provide protection and guidance.

The word *angel* means "messenger of God." These beings help us hear the messages of God's will, especially during times when we're in crisis or too frightened or stressed to hear the Divine directly. After all, our Creator is 100 percent love, which is the highest vibrational level of all.

It's easy to connect with God when you're in a state of bliss, such as during meditation. However, when you need heaven the most, your stress vibrations lower your ability to hear this voice from above. That's when angels are sent to your side, as bridges between the earthly ego and the Divine higher self.

Angel experiences come in many varieties, and in this book you'll read about people who have:

- Seen an angel either in meditation or with their physical eyes

- Met a person who appeared suddenly in order to rescue them or deliver an important message, and then the helpful stranger disappeared without a trace

- Had a dream-time encounter with an angel, departed loved one, or ascended master (for example, Jesus, a saint, or some other spiritual being) while they were sleeping

- Heard a voice that offered a lifesaving message

- Saw a vision or sign that proved timely and significant

- Had a strong intuitive feeling that led them to safety

- Received an idea or thought that was instrumental in providing protection

As you read *Saved by an Angel*, you'll likely notice more of the interactions you have with your *own* guardian angels. Since your angels are with you every moment of every day, you're continuously interfacing with them. So, your sensitivity to, and awareness of, these encounters will be heightened by reading about other people's experiences.

My prayer is that we will all remember to call upon our guardian angels. Our lives became more joyous, peaceful, and secure once we begin regularly connecting with heaven. We lose old fears about the future or about mortality, and begin focusing upon living life to its fullest. We worry less and feel happy more, knowing that our guardian angels are watching over us.

The angels aren't shy, and they want us to know that they are with us. Because we have free will, they can only intervene if we give them permission in some way—by praying or asking for assistance, for instance, or through visualizations or affirmations. When we give our angels permission to help us, we *all* benefit. After all, when we're at peace, we add more peace to the world.

I can imagine a world filled with happy people who are individually connecting with God and their angels. Now that's truly peace on Earth!

With love,

Doreen

PART 1

True Accounts

of People Who Have

Had Experiences

with Angels*

***Author's Note:** Certain individuals have requested anonymity, or that only their first name or initials be used to identify them.

Chapter 1

SAVED BY AN ANGEL

A WARNING VISION

by D. Sorensen

It was in the early '90s that I had a clear, lifesaving vision, with angels from above lending a helping hand.

It was an early summer's morning in Sweden. My boyfriend and I were driving near our home on a small gravel road. All of a sudden I said to him, "I think you need to slow down because my co-worker Kenneth is running late."

I had a clear vision of crashing with Kenneth and being flung out through the windshield, as I wasn't wearing my seat belt (it was unusual for me not to do so, but I guess I thought we were safe on the back roads). I saw the blood, saw myself flying through the windshield, and heard my boyfriend's screams . . . the vision was so vivid and eerie. In a hurry I put on my seat belt.

My boyfriend looked at me, said "Okay," and slowed down. He was familiar with my visions and knew that my instincts were almost never wrong, so he heeded my advice and drove 30 miles per hour instead of 40-plus.

Sure enough, no more than five seconds later, around the corner came my co-worker racing up the gravel road. We pulled off to the side as much as possible, but it was a narrow road with a barrier to our right, so there was no way to get out of his path. Kenneth was driving too fast, and he slammed on his brakes, but he still hit us, moving us some 80 feet up the road. We were in a Volvo, which was a write-off and undrivable after the impact.

I broke three ribs (due to the seat belt) and smashed my knees on the dashboard, as well as endured severe whiplash. But I remain forever grateful, as the vision saved my life, for sure. I've had many smaller visions since, but this one was the clearest and was no doubt lifesaving. I can only thank my guardian angels above.

～～～

An Angelic Buffer
by Nelly Coneway

May 15, 2008, is a day I will always remember.

In the evening I went to dinner with three friends, and at around 6:20 we left the restaurant. The crosswalk sign said WALK, there were no cars around, and we started crossing the street.

Suddenly a bright golden light blinded me—it appeared right in front of me, and time stood still. For the first time in my life, with my eyes open, I saw Archangel Michael and Jesus next to me. It felt very crowded on my left side. I looked over, but there weren't any people—just the energy field, which was thick, like a buffer between me and the approaching huge black monster that was so close, and yet so far away from me. My brain refused to register what was happening. I'd never experienced anything like it before and couldn't understand it: my physical body was there; but my spirit was far, far away, as if I was being teleported with the angels. . . .

I looked again at the oncoming vehicle—there were no sounds and I had no fear, like I was in another dimension. Then I heard people screaming and felt the angels lifting me up. As if in a dream, I watched in disbelief as a big black SUV sped away as fast as it could. For the first time, my brain realized that the SUV had just hit me and the driver had fled. I prayed that the angels help the police find the person—and then everything went black.

The next thing I remember was the police officer who came to the hospital in the middle of the night to tell me that they'd located the woman who had hit me and run away—which, according to him, was "a true miracle." Thanks to the angels, I survived the accident and healed, and the driver was brought to justice.

∾ ∾

"Zipper!"
by Bernadette Brighton

I was eight. The whole family and I had gone skiing. I was just a little one, so I was relegated to the bunny hill. They didn't use a chairlift on that particular slope, but rather an L-shaped conveyor. It was basically a horizontal plank of wood fastened to a metal pole. Skiers would just lean on the plank as it slid them up the hill.

I don't remember how, but I fell down while riding the lift. I was lovingly bundled up into a pink snowsuit—but this day it would be to my detriment. The hood of this one-piece suit got caught on the plank of the lift, and it started dragging me up the hill. I was choking, and my little life was flashing before my eyes. Of course, I couldn't get traction with my feet bound into the skis.

Suddenly, I heard a loud, booming voice shout, "Zipper!" It "clicked" instantly, and I undid the zipper of the suit, thus allowing me to breathe.

It took a few more moments for the operators to notice what was happening and stop the lift. They came to check on me, and I was frightened, as any child would be, but fine overall. I firmly believe my guardian angels saved me from suffocation that day, and for that I am eternally grateful.

I Feel the Source Within Me
by Deborah S. Nutile

To say that the angels changed or saved my life is an understatement! Four years ago I was living a life of hidden despair. Nothing made sense. I had everything—a "happy marriage," three wonderful boys, a beautiful home, a cottage in the woods, family, friends, work . . . yet inside I was miserable. No one knew of my pain. Every day I would put on my mask and go out into the world with a smile pasted on my face, just hoping to get through the day and get back into bed, where I would find my only relief. It was as if I were an actress in someone else's play.

One morning as I was standing in the bathroom getting ready for work, dreading yet another day, I said to God, "I know You are there in theory, but I can't *feel* You."

I suppose that was all the invitation that was needed, for what happened from then on has been absolutely miraculous. In the summer of 2008, I found myself at my cottage, immersed in the teachings of Eckhart Tolle's *A New Earth,* Dr. Wayne W. Dyer's *Change Your Thoughts—Change Your Life,* and *A Course in Miracles.* I was coming back to life again.

During this time I often went out on what I called my "angel ride" in nature. I'd always loved my angels and the signs they sent me: the number 111, butterflies, rainbows . . . these signs always made me feel so good. I hadn't had a lot of contact with my angels during my despair, but as I was becoming myself again, I was once more able to "see" them. So one morning as I was out on my angel ride, enjoying the beauty and serenity of the woods, I heard a voice say, "You need to write a book."

What? What was this? I'd never "heard" voices before, and I was very confused.

"You need to write a book," the voice repeated.

Write a book? How can I do that? I wondered. *I'm not a writer. And what would I write about anyway?*

The voice continued: "About your spiritual journey."

I was more confused than ever. I hardly felt like I was in a place to write about my journey. True, I'd come a long way since that day in my bathroom, but I really didn't feel as if I had anything to share. Yet I love my angels, so instead of completely dismissing this advice, I let it "sit" for a few days. It was an extraordinary time, and the "voice" was rather persistent. After the third day, I heard: "Don't fight it" . . . and I finally put pen to paper. You can imagine my surprise when about eight weeks and 500 handwritten pages later, I put down my pen and I had, in fact, written a book.

I have to say that it was one of the most incredible experiences of my life. My angels were with me night and day, and my life was changed in ways that have brought me to a place of pure happiness and joy! I've since continued on my journey and now find myself in the midst of other wonderful authors, including Esther and Jerry Hicks (The Teachings of Abraham®). Life is good . . . it is very, very good.

So yes, my angels saved my life, and they continue to guide me every day. I know they're always with me, and the best part about it all is that after just a few short years—and finding out about the Law of Attraction—I got exactly what I asked for that day in my bathroom. Now, not only do I know God is there; I *feel* God . . . I *feel* the Source within me just about every single moment of every single day. I asked and it was given! In four years, I went from a place of utter despair to being one of the happiest people on the planet, and I thank my angels daily as I stand in such vast appreciation for all that is!

CARRIED TO SAFETY
by Anna Martin

It was about seven years ago when I discovered that angels really do exist. I was driving to work via the day-care center. It was very early in the morning, very cold, and I had my baby in the backseat. As we were coming up to a little bridge, suddenly my windshield fogged up completely. I couldn't see out of any window, and there was nowhere to pull over on the bridge. I literally threw my hands up in the air and said, "Oh my God, someone is going to have to help me because I can't see a thing!"

Then it felt like my car was floating across the bridge and through an intersection on the other side, before parking safely on the side of the road. I believe angels carried us to safety that day. There is no other explanation. I sat there for some time, quite shaken, before I drove again—this time with a huge grin on my face.

AN ANGEL WAS WATCHING OVER ME
by Nicole Hume

I've always been open to angels and held a belief that there is something beyond our physical realm, but one day I became convinced that an angel was watching over me.

I live in New South Wales, Australia, and at this particular time I was working in the Blue Mountains, a very picturesque area. On my trip to work I would exceed the various posted speed limits, as I would nearly always be running late. The roads were wide and well marked, but on this particular day it was raining quite heavily and a mist had settled over the mountain. In my little car the windows fogged up easily, so I had to have the de-mister up high and keep wiping the windshield so I could see where I was going.

As you can imagine, driving in a mountainous area there are lots of bends and curves. I was coming into a 55-mile-per-hour stretch, which meant that I would have been traveling at around 65 miles per hour. I was heading around a medium-long bend to the right (in Australia, the steering wheel is on the right-hand side of the car), so I was limited as to what I could see ahead.

Then I felt as if someone kicked the back of my seat. There was a strange crackle that came from my stereo, and I saw a flash of white light and heard a voice tell me to slow down. I was a little unnerved, so I obeyed. Around the bend I came upon an accident that had just occurred that blocked the whole road . . . I had just enough time to stop!

I believe that I was being watched over, and if I hadn't received the message from my angel, I would have hit one of the vehicles head-on and been severely injured or even killed.

There's No Hiding from an Angel
by Sabine Vogt

I was about seven or eight years old, living in a little village in Germany. It was a nice sunny afternoon, and all the kids, including me, were out playing. A few of us decided to start a game of hide-and-seek, and we all tried to find a place where we would be hard to find.

Behind our house was a trash container only for paper, and I thought that this would be a great spot. So I climbed in and closed the lid. There was absolutely no way that anyone could find me.

Suddenly, the lid flew open and somebody grabbed me, and I had the feeling that I was flying out of the container. Then, once on the ground, I found myself staring at what I thought was a garbage man; however, it wasn't trash day, so the person had no reason to be there.

He stared back at me, and although it wasn't scary, I was so surprised that I ran away. It's safe to say that this angel saved my life, because I definitely wouldn't have been able to open the lid of the container by myself, and I could have suffocated.

So thank you very much, angel, for rescuing me!

∾ॐ∾

A Truly Special Awakening
by Anonymous

My angel story began last year. I moved to a beautiful new home, and soon after, I found Doreen's book *The Lightworker's Way*.

Upon reading this book, I had a truly special awakening, and the angels made their presence very clear to me in various ways. I could feel them through my heart center. I could sense them all around me for weeks, throughout every minute of the day. I could hear them singing—the loveliest sound I've ever heard. I could see them in my mind's eye. As I lay down to rest, the most beautiful colors would appear, guiding me through some intense and deep healing. I looked in the mirror, and for the first time I could see the very depths of my soul . . . the true beauty that was me, God's creation. So with the angels' guidance, I began my own spiritual journey.

I've been on this journey ever since and have made such positive changes. I've learned how to listen, and bring the angels' energy into my life and the lives of others through my art and the healing skills I've learned. Thanks to the wonderful wisdom shared in the book, I now know that I am a lightworker. I realize that it's no accident that I found it; that it was my time to wake up fully to my true purpose here on Earth.

What makes this story wonderful is that I was a real doubting Thomas who lived through pretty difficult life experiences, but now I have faith and healing that I can share. I will be eternally grateful for being awakened to my purpose, and to the angels energy that surrounds us daily.

∾ ∾

THE MOTOCROSS ANGEL
by Staci Christensen

Let me begin by saying that my husband, Travis, has been an "adrenaline junkie" since the day I met him. He enjoys all things fast, and loves to take risks.

I'd never really been too fearful, but I would avoid going to the motocross track when he and my son would ride their motorcycles. This was the first time I'd ever decided to see "my boys" ride. They were having a great time, and my two smaller children and I were watching from the fence line. There were just a few riders out on the track. Then Travis drove right in front of us around the first corner, hit a huge jump, and "cased it" into the ramp of the second jump.

At first it didn't really look as if he were hurt very badly. He stood and lifted his motorcycle up. He rested his head for a minute on the handlebars and then proceeded to try to start the bike.

All of a sudden I noticed a man sitting to the left of the jump, lounging in a lawn chair with an umbrella—I hadn't seen him there at all until that moment. He got up and told my husband that he would drive him back to where we had parked. He put Travis in the front seat of our truck and loaded my husband's and my son's motorcycles in the back, which I couldn't have done alone. Then he walked away. I can't even remember what he looked like, and I have no idea where he came from or where he went. But I was grateful for his help and drove on to the local hospital.

When we arrived, they x-rayed Travis and found that he'd broken every bone in the upper-left side of his body. They were afraid that his rib was so close to his aorta that it might puncture it, so they life-flighted him to the university hospital for surgery. When my husband was stable and starting his recovery process, he told me that he'd been helped by an angel.

I thought he meant this metaphorically; however, he told me that he *knew* that the man who had helped him out at the track was an angel. The man hadn't been there until that very second, and my husband and son had been riding for a while and knew everyone at the track.

An angel showed up that day, and we are truly grateful for the help heaven gave us!

AT THE ANGELS' INSISTENCE
by Luisa Wise

It had been several years since I'd had a cervical-screening checkup. Usually I went quite regularly, and I'd received letters from my doctor reminding me to book an appointment. But time passed, and I eventually forgot about it. Then one day in February 2007, I received another reminder letter, and as soon as I opened it, a voice told me that I had to go this time. The voice persisted until I made the appointment with my doctor . . . with good reason: my test revealed that I had precancerous cells, and I had to undergo treatment to remove them.

If I hadn't listened to that voice, I would either be fighting cancer . . . or I wouldn't be here at all. I thank God and the angels for warning me and insisting that I make that appointment. Now I'm fit and healthy, I go for my checkups every year, and I can expect to be here for my children and family for a long time to come.

CRADLED BY HEAVEN
by Renee Lukaszek

When I was 13, my family was going through a hard time. My dad had been into drugs and was an alcoholic. He and my mom would fight, and often there was physical abuse. The deeper into drugs and drinking my dad got, the worse things were at home. Mom was working two jobs to try to keep up with the bills. One night as she was heading out to her second job, things took a bad turn.

I was heating up the dinner that my mom had made for us earlier that day. My dad came home with one of his friends. They ended up getting high and were drinking heavily. My dad decided to take his friend home and made me go with them. I tried so hard to persuade him not to drive. I knew he shouldn't get behind the wheel. He yelled and told me to get into the car.

It was wintertime, and the roads were terrible that night. It was a long drive, and I lay in the backseat, just praying we'd make it safely to our destination. At one point I sat up and saw a dog up ahead on the road.

I said, "Dad, slow down! There's a dog in the middle of the street!"

He told me he didn't see any dog! It was then that I felt the softest hands cradling the sides of my face, like a gentle force pulling me back and laying me down on the seat. I couldn't understand what was happening, but I felt safe and protected. All of a sudden it was as if I were in a deep sleep. I remember falling off the backseat and hitting something hard. But as much as I tried, I couldn't open my eyes or move. It was like something was keeping me from seeing or feeling anything.

The next thing I knew, my dad was screaming at me to hang on and not die. It was still like I was in a deep sleep, but I could hear him faintly. He scooped me up and took me to the nearby home of a stranger, who witnessed everything!

It turned out that we were in a horrific car accident. At the last minute my dad had swerved to miss the dog and lost control. There wasn't anything left of the car. Dad said that the steering wheel had been pinned to his chest when he came to. He didn't know how he did it, but he pushed with all of his might and it moved just enough so he could squeeze his way out to get me. All three of us were hurt, but luckily there were no life-threatening injuries.

I truly believe it was my angel who not only protected us that night, but saved our lives. I think I might have panicked if I'd seen what was happening. I left the hospital with stitches in my face and a broken hand. Although I had to learn to use my right hand again, I know things could have been much worse. Dad got help for his addictions right after this accident.

I still have the scars to this day. It's a gentle reminder of my angel's presence and grace, and the love from heaven above!

THE VOICE THAT SAVED MY LITTLE GIRL
by Viki Gregory

One hot summer's day, my four girls, my sister, her son, and I had gone to the beach. I'd been injured with a third-degree sprain and was off work, and my sister was coming along to help me out with the little ones.

I'd just done the visual sweep. My third youngest, Cassie, who was three at the time, was playing in the shallow water with her older sisters; and the littlest ones were right beside my sister, who was making a sand mermaid. Feeling that all was safe, I'd begun watching my sister create her masterpiece when I heard a voice say, "Look."

Startled, I glanced at my sister's face, since I thought she'd been the one who had spoken. Then, as soon as I did, I heard a much louder, much more urgent "LOOK!" And when I looked up, there was my Cassie floating facedown in the water; her older sisters had gone to have fun in the deeper water.

I jumped up and ran, my heart pounding, not feeling anything . . . no pain, just my heart beating. I scooped Cassie up. She gasped for air and cried, "Mama, I was so scared! I couldn't breathe!" And I cried . . . I still cry, I am so blessed.

I am eternally grateful to that voice for saving my baby girl.

∽∾∾

PROTECTED BY AN ANGEL
by Jenn Krejci

I was probably ten years old, and my mom and I had gone to visit a friend and her daughter. It was our first time at their house. I remember that it had a long driveway, which was great because the other little girl and I spent most of the time outside with sidewalk chalk.

As we were coloring rainbows and hopscotch blocks, a yellow taxi drove up to the curb and stopped fast. The driver didn't get out, but he looked like he was in a hurry, glancing around and speaking quickly. He called out, "Hey, kid! You know where *mumble, mumble* Street is?"

I immediately felt someone very, very tall standing behind me, holding their hands in a crisscross position over my shoulders and torso. I couldn't speak. I couldn't move. My heart was beating very fast as my new friend took a few steps toward the taxi and asked, "What?!"

The taxi driver waved her closer. She walked a few more steps, and he repeated, "How do you get to *mumble, mumble* Street?"

She again asked, "What?!" and in my head I was screaming at her not to get close! *Bad! Bad! Run away! Why can't I move? I'll run to her and grab her, and we'll escape to the house! Why can't I scream for help?! Why can't I snap out of it and run to her?! No! Help! Danger!*

My friend got closer to the car, and I saw the taxi driver's door open a crack. At that moment my friend's mother peeked her head out of the front door. She yelled to the man, "Hey! Get out of here!" and called to her daughter to come into the house.

The taxi sped away with squealing tires that left black marks in the street. My heart stopped racing, and I felt the protective arms gently release me and disappear. I could suddenly speak and move again. It was as if I'd been frozen, and now I was *un*frozen!

I know now that if I'd run to grab my friend, we both likely would have been kidnapped. If I'd screamed for help, she probably would have immediately been snatched up. I'm sure an angel or spirit guide told that mother to check on her child—and luckily, she listened!

An Angelic Detour
by Terry Hibbs

I was on my motorcycle coming from Galveston, Texas. I was taking back roads instead of the interstate on my way to my cousin's house in Katy, outside of Houston, before heading home to Elgin, Texas.

I had my directions, and I came to an intersection where I thought I should turn, but something made me go straight instead. I'd gone a mile or so down the road before I realized that I had to backtrack because I had in fact needed to turn.

When I finally turned onto the correct road, I came upon a horrible wreck in the lane I was in. It had just happened minutes before. It occurred to me as I saw the police heading to the scene that it had been my angels who had guided me to go straight and then turned me back around when it was safe to do so. Given the severity of the accident I saw, and being on a motorcycle, I'm not sure that I would have made it. But I did . . . because of my angels.

As soon as I had this realization, I felt tingling throughout my body, and I teared up. All I could say was "Thank you, angels."

❧ ❧

THE CUSHION AND THE MAGNET
by Clara María del Carmen Mariaka Barríos

I was in my native country, Guatemala. It was November 2005, and I was traveling with my best friend to Guatemala City from Quetzaltenango, which is four hours away by car. We woke early because my friend had to be in a ceremony at 8 A.M. After three hours of driving, the highway grew straighter, but the condition of the road deteriorated.

Suddenly a pickup truck sped by and went in front of me (the highways in my country are only two lanes). My first reaction was to brake, and because of the condition of the road and the fact that my truck was empty, we started to roll. I can't remember the speed we were going, but I'm sure it was above 90 miles per hour. My friend, who had been napping in the passenger seat, was screaming at this point. My pickup rolled several times, and from the opposite direction I saw three big trucks coming toward us at a high speed.

At the moment I anticipated colliding with one of the trucks, everything happened in slow motion. I just closed my eyes, waiting for the impact . . . and then I felt "someone" pull my pickup from behind, and we landed in a cornfield. It was the season in Guatemala when corn is just harvested, and we ended up on a cushion of dry corn.

After the "landing," my friend and I hugged each other. Within a couple of minutes five or six men who had witnessed the accident came to the cornfield, trying to help us. They were asking if we were all right. From their point of view, the crash had looked devastating. They thought that we'd be dead and the car smashed . . . but nothing had happened! My friend and I were okay, without injury—only the emotional shock—and my truck was intact; the "cushion" had kept it from being destroyed.

All the men who helped us said that we'd disappeared from the road very quickly. It was as if a "magnet" had pulled my pickup away; otherwise, one of the big trucks would have hit us . . . and all of this had happened in the blink of an eye. My friend and I talked afterward, and we both described the same thing. We felt like "someone"—a major force—had pulled the truck off the road and into the cornfield.

It was a very dark time in my life, and I didn't understand it then, but now I know that Archangel Michael moved my truck, saving our lives! Everything finally made sense to me when I heard that angels don't intervene without our free will except when we're in dangerous situations. My first thought was of that accident.

∾∾

Into My Waiting Arms
by Claudine Lyell

On a beautiful day, my two children, my husband, and I arrived in Sydney, a two-hour trip from our home in the country. Our plan was that the kids and I would have a fun day in the city and then to go to the famous Luna Park amusement park that evening. My husband dropped us off at a train station, the kids and I rode a bus-train to the central station, and we proceeded to walk the distance to the center of the city.

We took our time strolling around, making our way to George Street, where we were surrounded by a mob of people. The kids seemed to pick up on the frantic energy of everyone rushing to and fro to get to their destinations. We came to an intersection where the traffic was stopped. The traffic lights in Sydney make a clicking noise when they change, so upon hearing this sound, my son proceeded to race across the road at a furious pace. Just at that moment, I realized that the light had turned green, signaling for the cars to go.

I became frozen with fear and shock as I realized that my son had just launched himself in front of about five lanes' worth of traffic. I screamed "No!" but was unable to move my feet—it felt as if everything just stood still. My son stopped halfway across the road and noticed that the cars were starting to take off. He looked at me, and I knew that this could be it: my son was about to be hit by a car at full force!

And then, I don't know how, but somehow he ran back into my waiting arms. I pressed him to my body. I wasn't going to let him go. We cried together as we both realized that he'd been given another chance to be here with us on this earth. I knew that by the grace of my guardian angel, he had "flown" across the intersection back to safety.

I looked across the street and found myself staring at the most beautiful church I'd ever seen. I didn't know its name. I just knew it as the beautiful church next door to the town hall in Sydney. When I Googled it, I discovered that it was called St. Andrew's Cathedral.

The biggest sign of all came as I was meditating on Christmas Day, 2010, and I was given the name Andrew. I asked, *Is there an angel Andrew?* and I heard the answer *yes.* I believe that St. Andrew or an angel called Andrew was looking after us that day, and his name came to me in meditation so that I would realize that he'd given me my son back. My husband and I are currently building a house, and I'm also convinced it's a sign that the address is St. Andrew's Way.

I believe in angels, and I believe there was one by my side that day in Sydney.

Lucky to Be Alive
by Jinelle Markham

The morning of December 29, 2009, was crisp, sunny, and clear. Lying in bed, still in the state in between sleep and wakefulness, I could hear my guardian angel talking to me. I couldn't make out what this voice was saying, however, and continued on with my day normally.

On my way to work late that morning, my younger sister called me and asked if I was okay, because she'd had a bad feeling about me. I said, "No, everything is fine," and didn't think anything of it. Little did I know her premonition was right.

As I exited the highway, my gas pedal stuck, which had never happened before. Nothing I tried would *un*stick it, and nothing was down there to block it either. So I slammed on my brakes right before I reached the train tracks. In a panic, I set my emergency brake, hoping that it would stop my car for a while. It didn't.

My car leaped onto the tracks uncontrollably. The next thing I knew, I looked to my left and a train was not even two feet from my face. It was about to broadside me going 30 miles per hour. The second I saw it, everything went dark. I instantly blacked out, before I was even hit. I believe the angels didn't want me to go through that traumatic experience, because it felt as if they pulled me from my body.

As I was waking up from my accident, still in my car, I felt as if I'd just come from—or was still in—heaven. My body felt magnificent and so at peace. Words are inadequate to describe how wonderful this feeling was. All I could see was white, and I could hear that same angel whom I'd awoken to earlier that morning again talking in my ear. I still couldn't understand a word of what was uttered, although it could have been something along the lines of "See, I told you not to go to work today!"—said in the most loving way, of course.

As I became more conscious, I realized there was a jacket over my body, because I think bystanders thought that I had died! But as

I finally came to, I felt pain, lots of pain. The ambulance was there shortly afterward.

I was extremely fortunate that day. I walked away (barely) with a dislocated shoulder, a broken collarbone, and a concussion. The recovery was very long and arduous; but I am very, very lucky to be alive.

I am eternally grateful to the angels for saving my life that day. Because of them, I'm able to say that I have a lifetime of greatness ahead of me to fulfill. I love you, angels. Thank you!

ASSISTANCE IN THE OCEAN
by Valerie Camozzi

I was planning a trip to Costa Rica with two friends. There were actually four of us—three adults and a nine-year-old. I went to a bookstore to look at the travel section prior to our departure. A book on Costa Rica fell from the top shelf onto the floor in front of me. When I picked it up, I found that it was opened to a page that gave advisory tips for swimmers in the ocean. It cautioned them about riptides.

I bought the book and brought it with me on our trip. After reading it, I was concerned about the nine-year-old swimming alone and made sure to tell everyone about possible riptides. I remembered reading specifically about what to do if caught in one, and shared this information.

Costa Rica was amazing, with diverse landscapes, tropical rain forests, sandy beaches, monkeys, frogs, and brightly colored birds. One day I went snorkeling with one of my friends. The water was incredible shades of aqua blue and perfectly clear, and the fish were abundant. We had been swimming for quite a while, and it was time to go back.

I saw my friend swim ahead until she was barely visible, and I began to panic when I realized I was swimming but not going anywhere. Thoughts of drowning entered my mind. I couldn't see my friend anymore—she was out of my sight. I tried to swim to the shore, but I was expending all of my energy and not getting any closer to it. I yelled and waved to people on the beach, but they were too far away.

A clear image of the travel book, and the page with the riptide warning and the paragraph with the instructions on what to do if caught in one, suddenly popped into my mind. But I was too tired from fighting the current to process the information. The fear of drowning and the realization that this was really happening opened the door for panic to take over.

It was then that I heard a male voice telling me precisely what to do. The directions were clear and direct. I followed them, and I made my way to the shore. Each instruction was repeated until I followed it. Once on the beach, I fell to the sand and stayed there until I had the energy to walk the miles back down to the part of the beach where my friends were.

I'm certain it was an angel who caught my attention with the travel book that fell off the shelf. I paid attention but required more help, and this angel assisted me in the ocean, directing me to safety. I feel very grateful. I know my life was saved by an angel.

Chapter 2

VISIONS OF ANGELS

THE GIFT OF THE ANGEL FEATHER
by Kate O'Rielly

It was 1998, and I was in the emergency room with a diagnosis of pneumonia. All the drugs used to combat this illness were given to me, and I was sent home with strict instructions on the importance of bed rest and taking my many medications. When I left the hospital, I felt I should really be staying, but there were no available beds. It appeared that, because of my age and general health, I would recover quickly on a homebound regime.

That evening, after I tossed and turned, kept awake by the sound of the vaporizer, I finally fell into a very deep sleep. At 3:33 A.M. exactly, I was woken up by some presence in my room. At first I thought one of the other members of my family was up moving about. When I turned over in bed, my heart began racing. There in my room were two very large bodies.

The two figures quickly made me understand without words that they were protecting me as I slept. I knew that they were angels. One of them was a male who stood about ten feet tall. But how could a ten-foot-tall figure fit in my room (which only had an eight-foot-high ceiling)? His robe was a very lovely blue gray, and he had a loving face that felt healing to me. The other angel was all white. Her energy was soft and nurturing. She reminded me of the angels I read about as a small child: half feathers and half human. I reached out to touch the angels and they were gone. I fell back into a restless sleep.

In the morning as I woke up, I became very excited about the "dream" I'd had. When my daughter and granddaughter came in to see how I was feeling, I told them about my visitation by the angels. My daughter was old enough to be skeptical, but my four-year-old granddaughter was awed and delighted by the story. After the excitement had passed, my daughter helped me out of bed to visit the restroom. At that moment, my granddaughter started screaming with excitement and glee. As I rose from the bed, a six-inch-long white feather came with me, stuck to my feverish leg!

The three of us didn't know what to think. I was very confused because there are no feather products in our home due to allergies. My daughter was speechless, and my granddaughter was dancing with joy because the angel had left a gift. She said she knew the dream wasn't really a dream, because angels visit people at night all the time. Of course it was an angel!

I carefully removed the precious feather from my leg and put it on my bedroom altar.

The next night, I felt that I was getting sicker, not better. I decided that if I didn't feel better soon, I would call my doctor. At 3:33 A.M., I was once again woken up by the feeling of a presence in my room. I turned over . . . and there were the angels again! As I watched them standing across from me, the male angel asked if I was ready to go with them to heaven. In many ways, I was overjoyed to hear them speak, and to invite me to join them.

The angels said they were there to help me decide whether or not I would stay living in my body. I thought about the projects I was working on, and about the unfinished business in my life. None of those things seemed more important than going with the angels. The love and contentment that they emanated was so appealing, and I wanted more of it. All of a sudden, though, I thought of my seven young grandchildren. If I left with the angels at that moment, I wouldn't even have a chance to say good-bye to them and receive a final kiss and hug. I told the angels that I wanted to stay on the Earth plane for now.

The angels told me that if I were choosing to stay, the only way I could remain alive was if I went back to the emergency room quickly. They disappeared as suddenly as they had come to me. As soon as possible, my oldest daughter took me to the hospital. As it turned out, the pneumonia had gotten much worse, and the doctors said that I'd made it to the hospital just in time.

The next morning at 3:33, I woke up, hoping to see my angels, but they weren't there. I wondered if moving to the hospital had confused them. I was very sad to think that I might not see them again, and I wondered how I might bring them back to me. I realized I should have asked them more questions. I felt that I'd missed an opportunity, and I questioned my decision not to go with them. I cried, feeling as if I were mourning friends I'd had for years.

My daughter and granddaughter came to visit me later that same morning. I hadn't talked any more about the angels since the feather incident. I was too weak, just focusing my energy on getting better. My daughter also had a lot on her mind, and I didn't want to burden or worry her. As we talked about my hospital experience, my daughter remembered something from earlier in the morning. She said *she* had woken up at 3:33, too, and had gotten a strong feeling about an important decision she was trying to make. She was very puzzled by the fact that she'd received such an insight in the middle of a sound sleep. But now her mind was made up—after many months of struggle, she finally knew what to do.

I smiled. My angels hadn't left after all; they were still with me and my loved ones. To this day, I cherish the gift of the angel feather.

The Powerful Love of Our Angels
by Anonymous

I was working as an assistant teacher. We were all sitting in a large circle on the first day of school, participating in an exercise designed to allow us to get to know one another. We would go around the circle, and everyone would share something about themselves. I'd already had my turn, and as it came time for the turn of a woman who was just a little to the left of me, I saw two angels.

As she began to speak, I saw what at first looked like the heat waves that rise above a blacktop on a sweltering day. The air above and around her seemed to move in this way, and then it turned into multiple colors, and then massive blue wings—two sets. I could then see the formation of beings attached. There were two of them, coming down on both sides of her. If she would have raised her hand, her whole arm would have been inside them.

This all happened in a split second, and I did sort of a double take, and of course as I brought my conscious awareness back to what was happening, I could no longer see them. But I was so stunned. It was like those old *Bewitched* episodes where everyone freezes, except *I* was the one who was frozen as everyone else continued talking. I couldn't hear a word they were saying. It was like I was just suspended in time for a moment, trying to catch my breath, still in the same vibration as these miraculous, beautiful beings; and even though I couldn't see them anymore, I could feel the tremendous love that the angels had for this woman.

I've only told this story to a few people, and the retelling of it does not do justice to the actual event. It is extremely difficult to re-create the feelings of this experience. In fact, as I sit here recalling it, I am moved to tears by the knowledge that we all have angels around us, and that they love us more than words can say.

Feeling Safe Again
by Greta Guldemont

I was a victim of a brutal rape. My unknown attacker broke into my apartment late at night while I was sleeping. Two years later, even though I had moved out of state and was now living with my husband, I suffered from terrible nightmares where bad people were chasing me and trying to hurt me. I would awake exhausted nearly every morning.

One night before Christmas, I watched *Miracle on 34th Street,* and later I was having a dream about the movie when I heard a voice ask me, "Are you all right?" It was a man's voice, and his words filled my body with an incredible warmth and peacefulness. I opened my eyes and saw a male figure at the foot of our bed. (My husband was sleeping beside me.)

Ordinarily, the sight of a strange man in my bedroom probably would have filled me with terror (as a result of my rape experience). But I just lay there, as peaceful and happy as could be, still enjoying the feeling of warmth throughout my body. He repeated his words, asking me if I was all right, and again I felt that incredible warmth through my body as I said yes.

He said that he was watching over me, and I remember smiling and then drifting off into the most wonderful deep, healing sleep. Was my heavenly visitor an angel, or was he the spirit of my dad, who had died when I was a baby? Regardless, I had *no* more nightmares after that! I've been so grateful for this experience.

∽∽

An Angelic Coach
by Terri Walker

My 11-year-old son, Steven, decided to join a baseball team over the summer, after playing soccer for several years. Most of the boys on his team had played the sport for years and were very good. Steven did pretty well, but he would freeze up at the plate and wouldn't swing at the ball. So needless to say, he would strike out a lot. We would take him to the batting cages, and he would do great, but during the game he would lose his nerve.

I was sitting in the bleachers watching my son play one day. Steven had already struck out twice and was getting ready to go up to the plate again. I noticed how his self-esteem was hitting rock bottom, and I wanted him to hit the ball so much. I decided to ask his angels to help him do so and get to first base.

Just at that moment, I saw an angelic being leaning over Steven's shoulder while he was standing at the plate. This angel looked right up at me and gave me a thumbs-up and a beautiful smile. I couldn't believe what I'd just witnessed! I looked around me to see if anyone else had noticed this angel, but no one seemed to.

The next moment, I heard a *whack!* Steven had struck the ball, and it flew between first base and second, straight down into right field. He made it to second base, stole third, and then ran home. The look of joy on his face was priceless! He was so proud of himself.

After the game, I told him about the angel, and he said, "I knew something wonderful happened because I felt that something was holding the bat, and I heard someone tell me to 'swing,' and I did!"

It just goes to show that the angels really *do* want to help, and that all you need to do is ask. Now, Steven talks to his angels all the time.

∞∞

TARA, MY HEALING ANGEL
by Robin Ann Powell

It was sometime in late November 1998 when a dear friend sent me Doreen's audio program *Healing with the Angels*. I was excited, since my health was going downhill. It seemed like all the healing methods I tried would only work for about six months. Angels were merely pretty objects to me prior to receiving the tape. I had angel decorations, given to me as gifts, all over the house, but I had never experienced actually seeing them or hearing them or receiving a healing from them.

I remember when listening to Doreen's audio book the first time that I fell asleep after about 30 minutes, and nothing unusual happened. About three weeks later, my kidneys were hurting me. A year prior to this time, I'd had a bladder infection that I just couldn't shake. It turned into a serious kidney infection, and I had to take antibiotics to bring the fever down. The infection finally left my body. So, here it was December 12, 1998, and my kidneys were hurting me again.

My husband and I weren't getting along that morning, so I asked him to sit down on the couch with me before I went to work. We got peaceful, and I had my eyes closed. Within a few moments, I saw this beautiful being. She had long black hair and was wearing a long white dress. She told me that her name was Tara and that she was going to put the palms of her hands—fingers extended—on my kidneys all day. This was going to happen while I was selling shoes at the department store where I worked. She also told me that I was an earth angel. I opened my eyes in great astonishment.

I told my husband what had just occurred, and we sat there, stunned. Was this a real experience, or my imagination? I went to work with great anticipation, hopeful that Tara would heal my kidneys. Within a few hours, the pain was gone!

It has been over a year now, the pain in my kidneys has never come back, and I know that it never will! I'm sure that listening to Doreen's tape helped me bring my angel to me.

Angelica
by Charles F. Turpin

One Friday night at my job, I walked up the six flights of stairs to the small protected area where I work with machinery. Out of the blue, I felt a sharp pain in my chest, so I lay my head down on my desk. But the pain grew until it was hurting a lot. I tried calling my co-worker downstairs for help, but he didn't answer.

Then I happened to look out the window and saw a person—a woman. She didn't resemble anything I had seen in church or on TV. She was outside the window of my work area 60 feet above the ground!

Her eyes were sparkling blue—not like any blue you could paint, and not like anything in a science-fiction movie, but beautiful. She didn't have on the kind of robe you always picture on angels; she was naked. But her skin was as white as I had ever seen—so white that the details of her body were hidden.

Her hair was red, long, and fluttering as her wings slowly flapped. The wings weren't like a dove's, but more akin to a sparrow's.

She never said hello, and she never had a glow around her, like in the movies. She was a real live being or soul. I tried to raise my head, but she came to me and laid her hand on it and turned my neck to where I could see her better. She just looked at me. She didn't speak through her lips, but through her mind. She said, "It isn't time yet." Then for some reason, I just happened to ask her, "What's your name?" and she said, "Angelica."

It seemed like I blinked my eyes, and then it was time to go. I drove myself home, and my wife took me to the hospital. The tests showed that I'd had a heart attack that evening. But they did another test the following Monday, and it showed that my heart was miraculously undamaged. Since then, I've also survived cancer even though I only had a 10 percent chance of living. Somehow I feel that Angelica is still around, helping me to survive.

My Life~Purpose Angel
by Pia Wilson

I had been meditating and trying some automatic writing to get to know my guardian angels better. I learned that the one helping me fulfill my life purpose was named Jim. At the time, I was feeling that my ambitions wouldn't amount to anything, and I was very frustrated. I accused Jim of not working hard enough on my behalf.

That night I had a dream. It was one of those dreams that feels more than real. In it, I was talking to a human friend of mine whose name is also Jim. I was joking with him, the way I normally would in life, but he wasn't responding appropriately. I got angry with him . . . then I noticed something. His eyes were quite different. And although on the surface he looked like my friend Jim, he was actually someone else. His eyes were wider and took up more of his face, and his cheekbones were particularly high.

I realized that this was my angel Jim, which explained the lack of humor. Through my meditations and automatic writing, I've come to know that Angel Jim is very serious. He took me to a room where there were hundreds of "people" sitting at computer terminals. Jim was showing me how many angels were working with him to help me fulfill my life purpose.

In the last few months, Jim has continued to appear to me in my dreams around the periods when I have made strides in my career. I always feel especially good after a dream involving him, and he's even led the way for my romance angel to use my dreams to communicate with me. Angels are wonderful sources of love, guidance, and advice. I can't imagine life without them now.

Angel on the Highway
by Perry Koob

It was 1966, and I was 18, living in Los Angeles. I wasn't in school, as I'd been kicked out for fighting the year before. I was pumping gas for work and had very few prospects. When my stepfather asked me to help my mother run a small farm in Missouri, I said I didn't have anything else to do, so sure, I would do it.

I gave notice, and two weeks later, I set out on a trip halfway across the country, driving a Corvair that my stepfather had bought me for the trip. It was equipped with a one-wheel trailer loaded with some things I was to take back to my mother.

There wasn't a 55-mile-per-hour limit, and I was taking full advantage of that fact. I was doing 80 to 90, and when I would brake, the taillights would make the trailer tarp glow red. I was going down a very steep grade and had to keep my foot on the brake. I glanced in the rearview mirror, and I saw what seemed to be a woman sitting there on the trailer, smiling at me. I looked back to the road quickly. I then rolled down the window, thinking that the cold wind on my face would snap me back to my senses.

I looked back in the mirror, put my foot on the brake again, and there she was. I could see her clearly in the taillights, although the light was red. She was dressed in a long flowing gown, and her head was covered with a shawl. She was still smiling at me, and then she waved. I thought, *Perry, you've finally gone off the deep end for sure now.*

I gathered as much of my courage as I could and pulled off to the side of the road just before a sharp curve. I put my head on the wheel, gritted my teeth, and got out of the car. As soon as my feet hit the ground, I fell down. It turned out that the road was all one big patch of ice! I got up, hanging on to the side of the car, and walked—or rather, slid—back to the trailer. I lifted the tarp under the trailer, but there was nobody there. This shook me up, to say the least.

Just then, the moon, which had been behind some clouds, broke through and shone down on the desert below. The moonlight allowed me to see about ten crosses all in a neat row, marking the places where people had gone off the road and been killed.

To this day, I look for that beautiful lady. I used to feel her beside me, but I no longer do, and I miss her being there.

∾ ∾

THE ANGEL WHO TUCKED ME IN
by Angie Chiste

In 1986, when I was 18, I got a job as a waitress at an all-night truck stop in a small Canadian hamlet, far away from my family. Our staff accommodations were located in an old hotel. We each had our own room, with doors that locked automatically when you closed them, like most hotel rooms.

One morning, I got off at 6 after working all night. I went to my room to get some sleep. I was so tired that I lay down on my bed, still in my uniform, without taking my shoes off. Sometime later, I awoke to the feeling of my shoes being slipped off. I lifted my head and saw a transparent lady engulfed in light. She took off my shoes and gently covered me with a blanket. I lay back, knowing she would watch over me while I slept. I wasn't scared at all.

When I awoke, I was under the covers, my shoes neatly in the corner. I knew no one had come into my room, as the door had automatically locked when I shut it. It was an angel taking care of me after a long shift at work.

∾ ∾

THE DAY I SAW THE ANGELS
by Laura Weintraub

It was a usual Tuesday morning, and I was getting the kids ready for school. My son Aaron was the sleepy bear of the family, and I generally had difficulty dragging him out of bed. He is always the first to get my attention because he starts school an hour before my other son, Alexander.

By the time Aaron got downstairs on this particular morning, he barely had ten minutes for breakfast. Mornings have always been tough for him; it's as if he's dragging a boulder behind him. To top it off, Aaron started in on Alexander, teasing him and goading him.

I had recently been studying *A Course in Miracles,* and I was learning a lot about myself and others. I watched how my children constantly provoked one another, always trying to best the other. I started to talk to Aaron, asking him why he was teasing Alexander. It was as if he was taking his frustrations out on him! Aaron started to tell me about school and how he felt that the other kids didn't like him. I've found that when one of my sons is feeling upset inside, he has a tendency to take it out on his brother, so I tried to help Aaron see what might be causing the problem.

Just then, my husband stormed into the kitchen, and he snapped at me to hurry up and get Aaron to school. I immediately felt like I was being attacked, and I allowed myself to feel hurt. I went to my room and cried. Then it dawned on me that I was *choosing* to feel attacked and to get my feelings hurt. If I chose to perceive my husband's actions differently, I could have a different outcome. I realized that I could change my perceptions anytime I wanted. It took me a couple of hours to forgive my husband and let go, but I did because I didn't want to feel this way the rest of the day.

I started to pray and meditate. I asked God to bring peace to me and my family; and to help me forgive my husband, my kids, and most of all, myself. I had to let go and allow them to learn their lessons on their own, trusting that God and the angels were with them, too! I no longer needed to feel that I had to be in control of everything.

As I sat and prayed in my room, I suddenly heard a tap on the window. I thought it was a bird or something. To my amazement, though, I saw that the sky was filled with angels! They were everywhere. I started to cry with joy. I truly wanted to see angels, and I really didn't know when or where it was going to happen. I realized that I had to be completely free and clear from all "attack" thoughts in order to experience their presence. I realized that they are all around us in everything we see, and that we are all one!

That afternoon, Alexander and I stopped at the drive-through to get an after-school snack. I was singing a song on the radio when my son said, "Mom, there's a face looking at me!" He pointed his finger to the sky. "Is that an angel?" he asked. As I sat in amazement, Alexander exclaimed, "And there's another, and another, and another!"

"Yes!" I agreed, as tears rolled down my face. It was a miracle. He was seeing exactly what I'd seen earlier that day.

Alexander was so excited and said, "I can't wait to tell Aaron. But what if he doesn't believe me?"

I told him not to worry, and I said a little prayer, "Please, Aaron, don't tease him this time!" As soon as we got home, Alexander raced up the stairs to tell his brother. I heard him say, "Aaron, guess what? I saw an angel looking at me, and then I saw three more!"

Then Aaron gently patted him on the back, and he simply said, "That's cool, man!" I smiled, tears running down my face, as they gave each other a big hug.

That was a special day—one I will always remember. It was the day I saw the angels! From then on, I was constantly aware of their presence; Divine love; and protection for me, my family, and all of us.

HOW AN ANGEL HELPED ME FIND MY TRUE NAME
by Uma Bacso

I hadn't liked my name, Nancy Jane, my entire life—as far back as I remember. I tried Nan, NJ, Nancy, Nanny. Nothing felt like "me."

One day I decided to meditate on the topic as I stood in front of my bedroom mirror. After some time meditating with my eyes closed, I decided to do an open-eyed meditation, and I saw a beautiful woman with long dark hair standing before me in the mirror. I asked this woman, "What is your name? What is your name?"

I heard her say, "Your name will have something to do with light." (At the time I had light hair.) I stayed seated for a short while after hearing that; then I proceeded to get dressed. One minute later, my body started moving over to my bookshelf, and I heard the woman say to me, "Your name will be in one of these books."

I felt my arm lift up as I was walking over to the bookshelf. It was now fully extended, and I picked up the book right in front of my hand. It was *Autobiography of a Yogi*, by Paramahansa Yogananda. I flipped through the book, and the name Uma seemed to stand out several times. I thought, *What a strange name.*

A few hours later, I went to yoga class and asked the teacher, "What does *Uma* mean in Sanskrit?"

He said that Uma was the "goddess of the rising sun." I was taken aback for a moment as I remembered that the woman in the mirror had told me that my new name would be related to light. At that moment, I fell in love with my new name: Uma.

A GREAT HEALING DURING A TIME OF GRIEF
by Jennifer Helvey-Davis

I was very close to my grandmother as I grew up. My mother was a single mom, so there were many times when I actually lived with my grandma. You could definitely call her a stabilizing factor in my life, and she was always there for me.

When I was 19, I moved back in with her and my grandfather. One night when I was 21, I had a horrible dream about a snake in my bed. It was so bad that I woke my grandmother up and made her come sit on my bed while I fell back asleep. The next morning, I found her dead on the couch. The event was extremely traumatic, and I was overwhelmed with grief.

While on my knees visiting my grandma's grave site, I looked up to the sky and cursed God. I told Him that I wanted my grandma back. The sky was slightly cloudy, and my eyes stung painfully from all of the crying I had done.

At that moment, this "thing" appeared in front of the clouds. It was like a starburst coming out from the center, yet it was gray, almost the same color as the clouds themselves. I was certain that my eyes were playing tricks on me. As I got to my feet, an image appeared out of the starburst, and it stole the breath from my chest.

The being had long hair parted in the middle and a distinct heavy robe with a cord around the waist. Its hands were outstretched from its sides, with the palms facing upward. I couldn't see a face, yet majestic wings pointed straight toward the heavens, and they appeared solid and strong. I felt faint, and I fell to my knees and whispered, "You are real . . . you are here."

It was the most powerful being I have ever seen. Standing in the middle of the starburst, this figure made me feel as if it had a lot of influence over my life. I was afraid, yet amazed at the same time.

Although the features of the being were hard to discern, I knew it was an angel. The wings and the hands made this fact very obvious to me. Now, I whispered, "You are an angel." As the tears spilled from my eyes, I could hardly believe what I was seeing. The angel acknowledged my presence and nodded to me.

With miraculous speed, its wings snapped back to its sides. They were fast and strong and made a loud *whoosh!* as they did this. The noise frightened me, but I didn't move an inch. If this angel had been on the ground, it would have been at least seven feel tall, and the wings would have been even more enormous than that.

The scene was so overwhelmingly intense that I finally had to tear my eyes away. When I looked back at the clouds, there was only the starburst shape, but no angel. I tried to squint harder, but my eyes were so sore from all of my crying. I looked over at the plot where my grandma was buried, and it seemed as if the grass there formed a shape. It was darker in some places than in others. When I looked really hard, I could see the shape of the angel in the grass.

I dropped the silk rose that I had brought for my grandmother onto the image of the angel, knowing that my grandma was in the mystical place that the angel had come from. Completely stunned by what had happened, I walked back to the car and scrawled a picture of the angel on a piece of paper. I left the cemetery with a strange feeling of calm and peace that I had not experienced since before Grandma's death. I often doodle pictures of that angel when I am feeling stressed or need comfort, and it always cheers me up.

∾∾

An Angelic Vision of Motherhood
by Sharon Blott

At age 27, I was going through a very difficult time in my life. I was depressed, a six-year relationship that I'd put all my hopes and dreams into had ended, and I had no direction. I remember saying to my mother that I felt dead inside, and I doubted whether that feeling would ever go away. I was also in the middle of graduate school and had recently been told that I would never be able to have children.

My mother asked me to join her and my sister and brother-in-law on a two-week vacation in Cabo San Lucas, Baja California—her treat. At first I declined, but she insisted, and so off I went. The first week was fairly uneventful, but it was a welcome relief to be away from my normal surroundings.

However, during the second week in Mexico, I had what I can only describe as a profound spiritual experience. One night while I was on the beach during high tide and a full moon, the skies simply opened up above me, and I was engulfed in a glorious golden light that radiated a warmth and love that I have never experienced in this lifetime. I saw and heard the angels, and there was sweet music playing. The angels were beings of great radiance, with long white hair, and there seemed to be hundreds around, but only two or so were really visible to me. The feelings they emanated were of love and peace, and were intense and fulfilling to the very depths of my soul.

My most profound recollection was of children's voices saying, "Mommy, Mommy," and calling to me. It must have only lasted a second or two, but it felt like an eternity, and I wanted it to continue forever. I felt as if I were finally home.

When I returned from my holiday, a trip to my doctor revealed that the condition preventing me from having children was gone. All my fears had disappeared, too; and suddenly material possessions had little or no meaning to me, and I had a difficult time being within my physical body.

I yearned for that feeling of home. Eight months later, I met my husband, and today we have two wonderful girls, ages six and two. I will never forget that they are my miracles, and that ten years ago, in Cabo San Lucas, I was reborn and forever changed by my experience. Two months ago I received a community newsletter that was advertising property for sale in Baja California. My husband and I bought a parcel of land—my dream come true.

Angora, the Angel of Peace
by Dianne SanClement

Most of my adult life, I've prayed that my angel would appear to me. When I was 45, I realized that I couldn't spend another day working at a job that left me feeling empty. I fantasized about leaving, and wondered how I could do so. I was married, we had a mortgage, and all of the reasons why I should stay played on and on in my mind.

At this same time, I found myself waking in the night to the sound of chimes ringing in my ears, and I would hear an angelic voice whispering, "Dianne, you did not come to Earth to work at and retire from the Boeing Company." I would lie there frozen, knowing in my heart of hearts that there was something much more important for me to accomplish. I knew that I had come here with a Divine plan, but I was scared because I didn't remember what that plan was.

The voices became louder, and I found myself reading books about angels. I decided to start journaling my thoughts and all of the messages I was receiving. It wasn't long before I knew that a power much greater than I was guiding me, and that I no longer had a choice. In order for my spirit to live, in order for my light to shine, I had no choice—I had to leave Boeing. The environment was suffocating my spirit.

On March 31, 1995, I walked away from my job, which no longer served me, without a clue as to what I was going to do. I prayed for guidance, and also prayed that I would learn to trust.

I began getting up each morning, journaling my thoughts, my fears, my joys, and whatever was on my mind. I could now sit quietly for as long as I wanted, and write. It was wonderful. It wasn't long before I found that information was coming to me via the paper I wrote on. I would go back and reread all that was written and be amazed. At first it startled me, just as the whispers in my ears had. And with time, I discovered that it was a joy, and that a relationship was forming with my angels. When the angels were done passing information on to me, they always ended with "Love and Light, Your Angels." I was never frightened by this experience, but I never told a soul.

A few years passed, and we moved to Camano Island, near Seattle. For the first time in my life, I was surrounded by trees, woods, and gardens. I had been in the city, surrounded by cement and tall buildings, for 48 years. I had always prayed that I would live in the country one day. I spent the first summer working in the yard with my hands in the dirt, and I loved it. I realized, as winter arrived, that I had spent five months in nature; and for the first time in my life, I had made a connection with Mother Earth. My husband and I even built an area where I could meditate and be close to all of the creatures, trees, and the wonderful earth.

On July 1, 1998, as I sat in my peaceful garden reading, I noticed something in my line of sight. There, standing 50 feet away, was a woman dressed in white, with long golden hair that sparkled. She even seemed to glow, and the field around her body vibrated. As I sat looking at her, she said, "Hello, my name is Angora. I am the Angel of Peace. I have much information to share with you."

With that, I jumped up, ran into the house, grabbed paper and pen, came back to the garden, and wrote down everything she told me. Hours passed by the time she said she would have to leave me, but not to worry, for she would be sure to wake me at 4:44. I was to have paper and pen ready and write down all that she said. I kept our date, and we have been in contact ever since.

Now, there are times when weeks pass before I remember to write. But Angora, bless her heart, is always there for me. I find that I spend a good deal of time in conversation with her. I can ask for assistance, and she guides me each step of the way. Angora has taught me a lot about the universe, and she has given me the gift of understanding. She has given me the strength to do and try things that I might not have tried in the past.

I have only seen her in form that one time. I am aware of her presence, I hear her in my head . . . and most important, I listen. I encourage *you* to open your heart and listen for that voice. The angels wait for your invitation. They love you. I urge you to trust and to open your arms, and you will receive their love and guidance.

Chapter 3

HELP FROM MYSTERIOUS STRANGERS

REST-AREA ANGELS
by Kathleen Smith

I was traveling on a rural highway very late at night. I'd needed to go to the bathroom for a long time but hadn't passed any businesses. When I came to a rest area, I really had no choice but to stop, and said a hurried prayer for protection. I entered the women's bathroom, and inside there was a large man in yellow rain gear: hood, pants, gloves, and boots. He said, "Oh, am I in the wrong bathroom?" and started walking toward me.

Then I smelled the strong scent of flowers and felt myself literally lifted up by what had to be an angel and "glided" out the door and to the curb. I was a bit astonished, but not afraid or upset.

At that moment a car drove up, and three couples got out. I was so relieved. I remember thinking that they must be incarnated angels . . . they were superthin, dark complected, and very well dressed; and they seemed to sparkle. They spoke a foreign language among themselves, and their voices were kind of high-pitched and melodious. I'd never heard anything like the language they were speaking. And their car was futuristic looking, not like any vehicle I'd ever seen. I think the angels *wanted* me to realize that this was a Divine intervention.

I saw the man in the rain gear on the far sidewalk—he must have left the women's restroom through the door on the opposite side. I felt completely calm and safe and went in the bathroom with the women. When we came out, the man in the rain gear was talking to one of the men, who nodded to me as I passed them on the way to my car.

I know that the man in the rain gear had intended to hurt me, but I have only positive feelings associated with this incident. I'd been through some difficult times during the holidays, and this experience gave me so much peace and hope about my future. I now know without a doubt that angels truly exist and that they do protect us. They can and do perform miracles, and they're able to save our lives. I feel so blessed and am now a lightworker, committed to helping others and the planet.

ॐ ॐ

ALEC'S GUARDIAN ANGEL
by Diane Bridges

When my son, Alec, was two years old, we were having some work done at our house. The workers asked if I would go down the hill to Duke's (an old-fashioned hamburger stand) to get them burgers. I took my husband's new car, which I was not used to driving. It had a gearshift between the seats. Alec came with me. When we got to Duke's, I left him in his car seat, locked the door, and went about ten feet up to the window to order the hamburgers.

All of a sudden, I saw Alec reach over and move the gearshift out of PARK. The car started rolling backward since Duke's was on an incline. I ran to the car, struggling to unlock it, but I couldn't stop it from rolling. All those stories you hear about mothers picking up boulders and trees resulting from a rush of adrenaline just didn't happen to me. I absolutely could not stop the car, and now it was out on Pacific Coast Highway.

I was hysterical, but still running alongside the car, trying to unlock it. All of a sudden, the car stopped with a jolt. I looked up, and there was a man holding the vehicle from behind. He told me to unlock the car, get in, and start the engine. I did what he said, pulled back into the parking lot, and immediately stopped to get out and thank him . . . but he was gone. I never saw where he came from or where he went!

$$\infty \infty$$

STRANGER ON AN ICY HIGHWAY
by Susan Daly

While retrieving a chain that had fallen off of his car, my husband, Clark, had slipped and fallen on an icy patch. After he managed to climb the hill to our house, he collapsed on our floor, writhing in agony. He had hurt his back during the fall.

I immediately called our HMO and asked for an ambulance to take him to the hospital. They said that they would be glad to send one, but if Clark had no significant injury, we would have to pay $500. Since I couldn't tell whether my husband's injury was "significant" and I didn't have that much money to spare, I decided to drive him myself; and my son, Scott, came along.

As we drove down a very busy stretch of freeway, Clark became nauseated, and I had to pull off onto the shoulder of the road. Afterward, I began the daunting task of merging back into traffic, which was moving at a fast clip. It was a very dark night, and as a space in the long line of headlights appeared, I began to maneuver into the lane only to find that I couldn't get traction in the snow! Scott opened the sliding door on the side of the van and tried to push us, but we sat with tires spinning, making no progress forward.

The empty spot in traffic had given way to another continuous string of headlights. I tried to get to an area where there might be more traction, but the van still didn't move! I put my head in my hands on the steering wheel and said, "God, I need help *now!*"

A moment later, a car stopped in the right lane of the freeway about ten feet behind my van. Its headlights were on, but not the emergency flasher lights that would warn other drivers that it was stopped. A long line of cars had come to a halt behind it. It was almost like a time warp, if you will, except that traffic continued to move in the other lanes. The road was slick, so for all those cars to just stop without accidents occurring was phenomenal. It would have even been miraculous if the pavement had been dry!

I saw a person get out of the stopped car. He appeared to be of average height, dressed in pants (probably jeans), a short jacket, gloves, and a stocking cap. I couldn't see any facial features, since the lights from the cars behind him only allowed me to see a shadow. Somehow I knew that he was there to help my son push, so I gave the engine gas and focused on getting the van moving to a point where we'd have enough traction to drive on our own.

As I felt the van's speed increase, I told my son to jump in, fearing that I would get stuck again if I stopped to pick him up. My concern about my son getting into a moving vehicle distracted my attention from the person helping him. Tasked with shifting gears and avoiding a guardrail, I had my hands full and couldn't open the window to thank our rescuer.

Later on, when I asked Scott if he had been able to thank the person who had helped him push, he said, "What are you talking about, Mom? There wasn't anyone helping me push the van. I did it all by myself!" At age 15, Scott was convinced that he was strong enough to have pushed the van on his own.

So many times I've wished that I could thank the person who helped get us back on the road, but I actually doubt that he was a person; I think he was an angel sent in response to my prayer for help. After all, it wasn't possible for someone to have seen our plight, stopped his car, gotten to the back of my van and pushed, and then returned to his own car in the time frame in which this incident occurred. How could all that have happened on a crowded, fast-moving freeway in icy weather, without there being an accident? The only possible answer is Divine intervention, an immediate response to my short, demanding prayer.

It turned out that Clark had suffered a compound spinal fracture. It was painful for a few weeks, and he had to wear a back brace, but he's fine today. And for that, we once again thank God.

THE HEAVENLY NANNY
by Catherine Lee

I saw and spoke to my oldest son's guardian angel. We were living in Lubbock, Texas, at the time. My son, Brandon, was two years old and was very adept at opening doors, latches, and locks.

It was a Sunday, and we were at church. We had taken Brandon to the nursery for his class. I was sitting on the couch in the foyer because I was in my eighth month of pregnancy, and the Sunday School chairs were uncomfortable. The foyer had large windows on either side of a double door. The entire wall was plate glass, covered with filmy curtains to let in filtered light. My husband was sitting with me on the couch when we noticed an older woman approaching, holding the hand of a small boy. As she opened the door, we realized that the small boy was Brandon.

The woman had white hair and a very pale complexion. Her suit was white with tiny black piping. She carried a white purse and had on matching shoes. She asked if this little boy belonged here at this church. For a moment, I was just too stunned to speak. She went on to say that she had seen him wandering down by the lake at the park behind the church and thought he might be in danger. Brandon would have had to escape through several doors and a latched gate to get off the church grounds.

I said that he was mine, and she handed him over and went out the door. I realized that I had not said "Thank you" and went out after her. She was gone. The sweet elderly woman had disappeared without a trace, just as mysteriously as she'd first appeared. Brandon is now 20 and a firefighter. I hope his sweet angel is still looking out for him.

THE ANGEL DOCTOR
by James R. Myshrall

On December 22, 1995, at 11 A.M., Hazel (my mother), Beverley (my wife), and I were involved in a car crash. In this accident there were two deaths, but there should have been four. My mother and the gentleman who caused the crash passed on. My wife smashed her kneecap and received a large cut on her forehead. My face was crushed from the eyes down. I was choking, drowning in my own blood.

Within seconds, a mysterious doctor and his wife appeared. He came through the windshield of our car, pinned me down (as I was thrashing around due to the head injury), and cleared the blood away, making it possible for me to breathe.

This unknown doctor prepped me for the ambulance to take me the great distance to a well-equipped hospital. Through various channels, I've tried to track him down, and I even attempted to do so through the TV series *Unsolved Mysteries,* but I've had no luck. I am unable to locate this doctor. There is no mention of his name in the police report. The only conclusion I can come up with is that he was an angel. I am alive and well due to this angel doctor.

I was told that my mother was killed instantaneously. I believe that she had requested that I not be taken away from Earth at this time, as it would be too much of a burden for my family.

AN ANGEL TO THE RESCUE
by Judy Garvey

I was driving to get groceries. I took my usual route to the main street when my truck suddenly stopped, and I drifted to the side of the road.

I retrieved my purse to walk to the main road, which had several businesses, where I hoped I could phone a roadside service. As I turned around and reached for the door, I saw a man dressed in security-guard clothes with a walkie-talkie coming around the corner, right toward me. He came up to my car window, asking if he could help. I said I was about to go someplace to call an emergency service. He said he could do that, and I heard him speaking on the walkie-talkie while I quickly looked in my purse for the roadside-assistance membership card. When I turned to thank the man for his timely help, he was gone! I looked up and down the street for him, but he wasn't there! The tow truck came almost immediately.

I started thinking about the circumstances of the incident, realizing that there were no business establishments in the area that would warrant a security guard, and also the fact that the man had come from around the corner and headed right to me. I knew that I'd had a wonderful blessing from a very real angel.

～～～

THE CAMP ANGEL
by Daniel R. Person

I was at Covenant Pines, a Christian family camp in McGregor, Minnesota, with my parents, brother, and sister. Every morning we had a mandatory church service. I was about seven years old and more interested in playing than going to church, so I told my mother I was sick and couldn't go. When everyone left, I went down to the lake to go swimming.

I was a poor swimmer and not allowed in the deep water. I thought that this was my chance, and I crossed under the H-shaped dock. After a minute, I swallowed some water and began to thrash. I struggled for a little while and went underwater. Looking up, I saw the light through the surface. I quit struggling and put my hand up out of the water as I went still and began to sink.

Just as my hand was about to go under, I shot up onto the dock. I was on my knees, throwing up at a man's feet. I looked up, and he asked if I was okay. I said yes, and he turned and walked away. I crawled off the dock and stayed on the beach for a little while. Then I walked back to my cabin when I felt better.

I slept the rest of that day and looked for the man at dinner that night. There were only about 70 people there, and I spent the rest of the weekend looking for him. He wasn't anywhere to be found. We were in the middle of nowhere, so he wouldn't have been there if not for the camp (or to save my life!).

SOMEONE SAVED MY LIFE TONIGHT
by Justine Lindsay

I was 18 and had just finished school (I live in Australia). Normally, this would be immensely exciting. However, I was awaiting my exam results, which scared the wits out of me. Even worse, I caught my boyfriend (and first love) kissing another girl at our prom, just days before we were due to go away on vacation together for a week.

That week's holiday was hell. We'd fight and fight and fight and then make up, only to fight again a few seconds later. It was awful. It came to a breaking point when he said some really harsh things to me, and I stormed out and headed straight for the beach. I've had a fairly rough childhood, and all of this was getting to me. Although I'm ashamed to say it now, the thought of killing myself was at the forefront of my mind.

I went to the deserted beach, and I began to walk toward a huge cliff. *My way out*, I thought. I was hysterical, crying, sobbing, and wailing. I couldn't see anyone around, but then again, I wasn't in any state to notice anyone else.

At that moment, I felt someone tap me on my shoulder. It was a man of about 25, well groomed, with translucent skin and beautiful blue eyes. He asked me if I was okay, but he transmitted these words somehow silently, because looking back, I cannot remember him ever uttering a word. I began to tell him everything—*everything*. We walked farther, me pouring my heart out to him all the while. We sat down and I continued, telling him everything that had happened to me since the age of 12, when my parents had divorced. As I kept talking, he gently guided me back toward the beach house I was staying in with my boyfriend. We reached the trail that would take me there from the beach.

He stopped and turned me toward him. I realized that I'd been talking nonstop for more than two hours. I began to apologize, and I thanked him for listening, all in the same breath. I told him that I should go because my boyfriend would be getting worried, and then I hugged him. He still didn't say anything, and I remember thinking that this was a little bizarre.

I turned to leave, ran up the beach a bit, and then turned around to wave good-bye. But when I looked back, the beach was empty. I walked back down to where I had just stood with him and looked around. Nothing. I closed my eyes, thinking I was going mad, and shook my head. When I opened my eyes, I saw that there was only one set of footprints trailing up the beach along the path this man and I had walked. I felt really weird at this point and ran back to the house. I never spoke a word of what happened that day on the beach to anyone.

I have become more of a spiritual person because of this occurrence, and I continue to search for more meaning in my life. I speak to my angel all the time, and although he hasn't "appeared" again, I have never been as desperate as I was on that day at the beach. I get little signs every now and again, but usually only when I ask for them.

ᖇᖇᖇ

Overflowing with Joy
by Nancy Kimes

The year was 1980. It was an unusually hot day in the middle of the summer, a day I will never forget! I was very depressed. Nothing seemed to be going right in my life, including a relationship I was desperately hanging on to. My life had no plan, no direction. I was looking for a way out, so I asked God for help. I needed to know that I was here for a reason. I wanted to be able to help myself and others. At the time, that wish didn't look very promising. I cried as I spoke to God, as if He were standing beside me.

Then there was a knock at my door. *Oh, who is that?* I thought. *Should I answer?* The knocks continued. I finally opened the door, with tearstains on my face. Before me stood a man around 30, handsome, with a bright smile and a clipboard under his arm. He was wearing a long-sleeved shirt and dark trousers. His sleeves were rolled up a few folds. He said he was sorry to bother me but wondered if he could have a glass of water. I couldn't refuse him, as it was hot as blazes out there. I asked him if he would like some ice, also, and he said, "Yes, that would be fine."

As I turned on the faucet, the heaviness I had felt seemed to be lightening. He finished his glass of water, and I asked him if he would like some more. He said yes, with much appreciation in his voice. So I poured him a second drink, again with ice. This time I started to feel like something was filling up inside of me. I noticed that my mood, my depression, was lifting. I was feeling better! The man finished his second drink, and I asked him if he would like another. He was still thirsty!

So, as before, I started to pour a third glass of water. I experienced an overflowing of joy, and spontaneously thought of a beautiful biblical scripture: "Those who thirst after righteousness . . . shall be filled."

Who is this man, and why is he having this profoundly positive effect on me? I suddenly wondered. He finished his water and seemed satisfied.

He thanked me warmly and left. As I shut the door, I felt a peaceful inner certainty that my answers would soon come, that I had a purpose and I wasn't finished here. I dashed to the kitchen window to see which direction the man had gone, but he was nowhere to be seen. He could not have disappeared from my view that fast! Then within the deepest part of me, I knew that he was an angel in disguise.

My life changed that day. A whole new world opened up to me— one of love, forgiveness, listening to others, seeing myself through others' eyes, and having the ability to help myself through helping others. Now that I think about it, whenever something happens and I find myself completely overwhelmed, I feel an unmistakable presence within or around me that gives me the strength and courage to face the challenge and move on, knowing that I will be fully protected.

∾∾

HEAVEN HELPED ME
by Carol Pizzi

On September 14, 1995, while driving to work, I started to experience a tightening in my chest and pain that was going up in my throat. Having already passed right by the hospital, I decided to try to make it to the office and have someone take me to the emergency room. However, after driving a few more blocks, I started to feel very weak and had to pull the car into a deserted strip-mall parking lot. This was all happening at around 6:50 A.M., and none of the stores were open.

Just then, a man appeared, and I asked him to call an ambulance, as I was continuing to have chest pains and trouble breathing. I remember him going into one of the stores to make the call. The ambulance came and took me to the hospital, where they performed a cardiac cauterization. After they found a blocked artery, I underwent angioplasty.

After spending time at home recuperating, I returned to the strip mall, trying to locate and thank the gentleman who had called the ambulance. Since I had seen him go into one of the stores before their opening hours, I figured he must work at one of them. All of the store managers told me that no one would be there at that time of the morning and that no one of that description worked for them. I could not find my guardian angel, but I'm sure that's who he was.

❧ ❧

It Pays to Pray
by Anonymous

It was an ordinary spring day, and my husband asked me to help move our older Pontiac Firebird out of the carport area, as it was blocked by a hedge and wasn't accessible to the truck that would tow it to the shop. As my husband pushed, I was to steer it out of the spot. Well, as he was pushing and I was steering, I found that he was unable to handle the job as he'd thought. His back was strained, and I was trying to steer the car while seated inside. I felt that I created more weight, so I decided to get out of the car and help push, too. The only problem was that I couldn't maneuver the vehicle and brake as well. This was an enormously unwieldy car—a 1976 Firebird has a lot of heavy metal—and we felt as if this was unbelievably hard to manage. Just as we would get the car to move, I would jump inside to brake before it hit my husband.

I started to pray in my heart, and I asked my angels to help me. While I was stating these requests inwardly, my husband was trying to push the car, which was going nowhere. Just as I was in the middle of my prayer, I looked up and saw the most interesting manifestation of my entire life. A man was running from what appeared to be the fence by my house. As I watched him come toward us, I noticed that he turned, almost as if he were feeling his way toward the car. When his loving eyes met mine, he nodded as if to say intuitively, "I am here!" He approached the car and started to help push it. My husband was totally shocked to see this man helping, but the two of them managed to push the car into place.

I hit the brakes and shifted into PARK. I noticed that the man— who had blond hair, blue eyes, and a beautiful golden-bronze tan all over—was shaking my husband's hand and saying something to him that I couldn't hear. That's when I got out of the car and walked over, just in time to see him turn and leave, running in the same direction he'd come from and disappearing from our sight.

Focusing on my husband, I noticed that his eyes were watering, and I asked if he was all right. He couldn't speak, but finally after a few seconds, he murmured that the love emanating from that man had been so incredible. I asked him what the man had said. My husband turned to look at me. "He said, 'It pays to pray.'"

We never saw the man again, but we have never forgotten this amazing and wondrous occurrence.

$$\approx \approx \approx$$

Chapter 4

HEALING MESSAGES FROM MYSTERIOUS STRANGERS

WILLIAM WHITE
by Dawn Elizabeth Allmandinger

In the 1980s, I was married to a man who physically abused me. We both worked at the same restaurant—I was a waitress, and he was a busboy. He would say mean things to me in front of my co-workers, and once I came into work with a black eye covered with heavy makeup.

One day, a man and woman whom I had never seen before entered the restaurant. The man started to ask me things about myself, and then he said that I was special. But at the time I didn't think that was true because my ex-husband had always told me otherwise, as had my father.

He asked me what I thought my mission in life was. Without thinking, I said, "Well, I'm God's helper." The man told me that not many people know that about themselves. He asked me how I thought I helped others. I told him that I hugged people, and I could feel what was going on inside of them.

He told me that I was right, and that I should give the woman who was with him (his sister) a hug and tell them what I felt. I hugged her, and I told her I felt she wasn't happy and that she was going through some kind of move that she was uneasy about. The woman confirmed that she *was* going through a move, wasn't sure if it was the right thing to do, and wasn't really happy about it. I couldn't believe that I had gotten it right!

The man told me that he felt I was a healer, which I had been told twice before, but I hadn't thought I was special enough. Now, these two people didn't know me from Adam, and the man seemed to know things about me and my life that no one did. He told me that I wouldn't be with my husband much longer, which at that time I didn't believe. I really thought of marriage as a "till death do us part" commitment.

The man then asked me if I wanted his phone number, and I said yes. What's strange about this is that the restaurant was really busy with the lunch rush, yet the only people seated in my section were the man and his sister. That gave me time to talk with them.

So, I opened my address book to a blank page, and he wrote: "William White, 758-6055." Then he said, "Look at my name. See, it says 'Will I Am'!" William asked me to call him so that I could join a group of helpers and healers.

A few days later, I dialed the number, and all I heard was a recording that said the number had been changed and that there was no new number.

I did end up divorcing my husband, as William predicted. I am now ready to forgive my dad for the abuse, as well as my ex-husband.

I have looked for William White ever since then, with no luck. I truly believe that he was an angel in human form trying to guide me back on the path to peace.

GOD WORKS IN MYSTERIOUS WAYS
by Patrice Karst

I was driving on Interstate 10, heading west toward Pacific Coast Highway, on a Saturday afternoon. I was listening to music, and my small son, Eli, was asleep in the backseat.

I was lost in thought when the car in front of me slammed on its brakes! I was going at least 50 miles per hour, and I hit the brakes hard in an attempt not to careen into the car. But it was obvious that there wasn't enough time to stop. It all seemed surreal as I found myself heading straight for the car in front of me at a high speed. It was terrifying! I was thinking, *Oh God, is this where I die? What about Eli? Oh God, please, no!*

I crashed into the car with a great impact. Afterward, I was shaking uncontrollably and was afraid to move, lest I be confronted with the horror of seeing blood, bodies, and glass everywhere. But when I summoned the courage to look around, instead of witnessing a tragedy, I saw a miraculous scene. My son, Eli, was still asleep! I was completely uninjured, which, considering how hard I'd hit the other car, seemed utterly impossible.

As I was considering this unlikely situation, a dark-haired woman with a very thick unrecognizable accent opened my door, and I stepped out of the car. She threw her arms around me and said these exact words: "We are all going too fast. You are fine. Let us remember to slow down." Then she said, "May God bless you!" and she got back in her own vehicle and drove off. I stood there in a state of shock.

My car was completely unscathed, yet I had just had a huge collision. Not only that, somehow my vehicle was parked safely on the right shoulder, completely out of harm's way, even though I hadn't driven it there! I'd never moved it after the crash. I should have been in the middle of the freeway, with cars swerving to avoid me.

Miracle? Angel? Call it what you want. I just know that the mysterious lady and that experience made no sense to me. *We are all going too fast.* Quite a metaphor for this crazy, intense pace we've set for ourselves. I got back in my car and slowly drove home. God was there that day for Eli and me—I'm certain of it.

～～

An Angel in New York City
by Anonymous

I decided to follow my fiancé (who soon became my husband) to the New York area in 1995. We settled in an apartment that we could afford in New Jersey. This proved disastrous. There were signs early on that this was not necessarily a good decision: I was involved in a head-on collision before our move; and other disasters included getting my car stolen the day I started my new job, and having men expose themselves to me on the various subway trains I would use to commute to Manhattan each day. All in all, my husband and I had our cars stolen four times within a one-year period.

Finally, my husband lost his job and couldn't find another one with comparable pay. He decided to move back to the Washington, D.C., area, which had a thriving job market. I remained in New York City until a job transfer came through for me. During this time, I lived with a friend in Manhattan.

One day a man approached me after I had parked on the street, and loudly exclaimed that I was in his parking space. My friend who was with me told the man that it was a public spot. The man became quite angry. Against my better judgment, I left my car there. My inner voice told me to drive away, but my friend convinced me that I needed to stand up for what was right and not let the guy bully me.

Later in the day, I returned alone to find that my car had a flat tire. Someone had taken a knife and slashed it repeatedly. I cracked. I knew that this was the result of the parking incident, since the man had threatened violence when I'd left the car earlier that day.

I drove my car, crying all the way, and called a roadside service to assist me in replacing the tire. I was totally hysterical at this point. The city had finally defeated me, and I felt hopeless.

After calling for assistance, I carefully scanned the area in all directions for the service truck that was on its way. I had parked in a somewhat secluded location that I considered safe because it had open areas where I could see people coming. I believed that the guy who had slashed my tire might have followed me.

Suddenly, I heard a woman's voice behind me asking about my car. I did not see this person approach and was quite startled because I had been vigilantly looking all around. Crying, I told her the story. She was very comforting the entire time, while listening intently. She said that God would not have put us all here if there wasn't room enough for everyone, and that He would always provide for me, be it a parking spot or anything else. She also told me that I would soon receive a great blessing that would heal the entire situation with my tire.

At that moment, I saw the service truck approach. A second later, I turned to thank the woman for being so kind, but she had completely disappeared! There wasn't anywhere she could have hidden and no building nearby she could have gone into. A great wave of happiness and comfort came over me at that time. I truly believe that the woman was an angel. There is no other explanation.

The blessing she told me about also came true. The very next day, I received an award for $50 from an employee-recognition program. This was the exact cost of replacing the tire that had been destroyed. In addition to that, it boosted my self-esteem! A true miracle had occurred during a time when I thought nothing good could happen.

"Everything Is Going to Be Okay"
by Dorothy Durand

My mother, Marjorie, told me a story about an incident that occurred when I was an infant.

Tragedy weighed heavily upon her. At age 22, she had lost her brother, her mother, and my father (who died at 31); and I was gravely ill. The doctors suggested a new therapy that had never been tried on infants. They gave me a 50-50 chance of success if she consented to the treatment. If she declined, I would surely die.

So my mother signed the consent form, walked out of the hospital, and went straight to the harbor, where she planned to drown herself. Everyone she had ever loved had been taken away from her. She believed I would die and that she had nothing to live for.

As she stood staring into the murky water, a black man who appeared to be a dock worker came up next to her. At first she was afraid because he was such a big man, and it was a rough neighborhood that women just didn't frequent. But then she thought, *It doesn't matter.*

He said, "Killing yourself is not the answer. Everything is going to be okay." My mother looked away from him for a few seconds and stared down into the water again. When she looked up, he was gone. She scanned the area, but the man had simply disappeared into thin air.

Everything *did* turn out okay, as I obviously lived. My mother had a special affinity with the angels from that time to the day they took her home . . . on May 18, 1999.

MEETING MY ANGEL
by Cammy Rosso

I attended Doreen Virtue's workshop here in Calgary, Canada, in October 1999. In the workshop, we were taught how to ask for our guardian angels' names. I discovered that my angels were named Teresa and Walter.

Two months later, on December 17, I had the most amazing encounter. I was working on a project at a seniors' drop-in center for a few hours. I was chatting with an elderly lady when a man walked in and sat down. We began talking, and he told me that he'd had several visits from his wife after she passed on, and that he thought she was trying to give him a message. I told him that I believed in angels, and he responded by saying, "I know you do!"

I felt so comfortable talking to this man I'd just met. He was so warm and caring and understanding. Before I knew it, I was telling him how my husband had been out of work since the previous March and how tough it was for us to support our two boys.

He just sat and listened, and at one point he put his hands on mine and told me, "Everything is going to be okay; it's all going to work out for you and your family. Keep doing what you're doing, and keep the faith. Things will get better. I know that it's a struggle right now, but it will work out, and you will get through this."

I had this feeling of peace that everything really *was* going to be okay as he spoke to me. Then the man said, "I'm going to tell you something, and you will know what I mean; you will understand what I say to you." He then told me that he loved me!

At this point, I felt like the whole world had stopped—just like in a movie—and no one else was in the room. I asked him, "What's your name?"

To my amazement, he told me that his name was Walter! At that exact moment, I had no doubt in my mind that I was sitting there face-to-face with my angel! I also had this most unreal feeling, like a thousand shooting stars going through the top of my head and right out my toes. I can't even begin to explain the love and warmth that I felt. I told him about the workshop and that my angels' names were Teresa and Walter. He smiled, and said to me, "Well, I guess we need to meet Teresa." I told him that I wanted to come back and visit again.

He told me not to worry and that we would meet again. Walter then took my hands in his. He again told me that everything was going to be all right and not to worry and said that he loved me. He gave me a big hug, kissed me on my left cheek, and told me to have a merry Christmas with my family and friends. Then he turned around and walked out of the room.

I stood there for a few moments trying to take it all in. I realized that the woman sitting at the table had gotten up at some point and had walked to the other end of the room. She returned to the table and rejoined me. I said to her, "That man was so amazing and kind. I want to come back and visit him again."

She looked at me and said, "Yes, he seemed very nice. It's funny. I've volunteered here every day for the past three years, and that's the first time I've seen him!"

༄ ༄

Dancing Angel Boy
by Jill Wellington Schaeff

The first time I heard the song "Hands," by pop singer Jewel, the words leaped from the radio, mesmerizing me with their wisdom. One line in particular, referencing kindness, squeezed my heart. Now, every time I hear the song, my physical surroundings blur, and the spiritual message takes over my very soul.

That's what happened in November of 1999, only the words didn't flow from the radio. My husband and I are Cub Scout den leaders, overseeing a rowdy group of six second-graders, including our son, Mark. We were asked to supply a Christmas-ornament project for at least 50 boys at the monthly pack meeting. The boys from eight different dens would move from table to table making the ornaments, then deliver them to various nursing homes in December.

It was also our den's turn to create a crafty neckerchief-slide project for the month of November for our pack's 88 Cub Scouts.

The inspiration came early one morning in a dream. I clearly saw the project laid out before me—a little ear of Indian corn, popcorn kernels glued to a corn-shaped piece of cardboard with straw poking out the top. It was adorable! I jumped out of bed and headed straight to the kitchen to duplicate the project from my dream.

I spent the entire day experimenting with food coloring to get the exact shades for Indian corn. It took hours to mix the colors, blend the kernels, and measure them into tiny plastic bathroom cups, one for each boy in our Cub Scout pack. My hands cramped as I painstakingly cut out 88 cardboard cornstalks and glued the straw on top. I then placed each one into a cup of popcorn kernels so that every boy would have a ready-to-make kit. Then he could glue on the kernels and complete a slide for his uniform's neckerchief.

I was proud as my family helped me carry the projects into the school gym and lay them out. Our long table was immediately surrounded by whooping boys from all the different Cub Scout dens, drawn to our neckerchief-slide project.

"Look at these neat little corns," I heard them saying.

Tiny hands reached for the boxes in front of me, plastic cups tipping over and spilling. "I have just enough for each boy in our own pack," I said, my mind flooding with frustration. What seemed so orderly in my house was now chaotic. Finally, the pack leader saved me by announcing that each boy must rotate from table to table. Our table remained the most crowded, with boys gathering around to make the little Indian corns.

As my husband and daughter guided the boys through the ornament project, I struggled to make sure we had enough supplies. "Honey, you only need *one* cup of popcorn," I said to one of the boys. "Try not to spill your cup; that's all I have," I told another. I was definitely feeling stressed.

During this confusion, a little boy danced over to me. Dressed in a long-sleeved plaid shirt, instead of the bright blue-and-gold Cub Scout uniform, the child appeared either Indian or Hispanic. "I want to make the little corn," he said, his brown eyes like full moons.

"Honey, you will make a project with your pack."

"Please, I want to make the little corn," he pleaded.

I felt overwhelmed with so much chatter, plus parents and other adults vying for my attention. Losing my patience, I asked, "Where is your Cub Scout den?"

He stared me right in the eye and said, "I don't have a den." The answer was vacant, confused. Kneeling down in front of him, I firmly told him that I only had enough corn projects for the Cub Scouts, but that if he could bring me his den leader, he could do the project. With that, he danced away, twirling around and around. I was relieved that his leader would deal with him.

That's when it happened. Inside my head, louder than the lively din echoing off the cement walls, I heard Jewel singing the lyrics about kindness being the only thing that matters. My heart suddenly swelled with love and remorse. As little boys tugged on my sleeve, impatient for me to demonstrate the corn project, I rose from my seat, my eyes brimming with tears. "Excuse me, I need to do something."

I quickly made my way through the crowd, searching for the dancing boy with the heavenly brown eyes. I wanted to find him and invite him to make a corn slide, just as he'd asked in his simple, sincere request to me. I thought that surely with his plaid shirt, the little boy would stand out among the sea of blue and gold.

But he was nowhere to be seen. I walked from table to table, my eyes searching each face. I started to quake as I scanned the length of each table in search of the dancing boy. He was not among them. Where was he? At that moment, I noticed a table with a group of physically and mentally challenged Cub Scouts.

Like a former Scrooge who'd had a huge awakening of the heart, I announced, "I want all these boys to come to my table. I have a project waiting for you."

Precious eyes lit up, and parents delighted in helping the boys with various physical limitations get across the crowded room. I seated the eight boys around the table, and watched in awe as they carefully glued the kernels to the cardboard.

My heart sang with joy the rest of the evening, as the boys slowly completed their projects. Just like the fish that multiplied in the Bible, my supplies for the corn project seemed to do the same. After all the boys had made their neckerchief slides, I still had several kits left over.

I continued to scan the room for the dancing boy, but he had disappeared. I know now that he was an angel, sent by God to teach me a tremendous lesson about kindness. The experience ignited a change in me. Whenever I feel frazzled and impatient over life's little stresses, I sing the inspiring words from Jewel's song to myself.

$\infty\infty$

A Messenger from Above
by Kimberly Miller

The first time I realized that I'd encountered an angel was in 1985 when my grandmother died suddenly from heart failure. She had been on dialysis for about five years, and during one of her treatments, she'd had a major heart attack. She was rushed to another hospital, and my father called me to tell me she was there.

Before I could even leave the house, he called again and told me she was gone. I was very close to my grandmother and was devastated. I was extremely upset and concerned that she had died alone.

We were at the funeral home for the visitation, and the oddest thing happened. A Dominican nun (the order of the nuns who taught at the Catholic school I had attended as a child) approached me. She touched my hand and said to me, "I was with your grandmother when she died. She told me to tell you that she is okay now and she knows how very much you loved her." I was so surprised that I was speechless for several minutes. I turned to thank her, and she was gone.

I asked my brothers and my father if they had spoken to the nun, and they looked at me strangely and wanted to know what I was talking about. Nobody in the room that day had seen her, let alone talked to her. I realized then that the angel had come to calm my fears about my grandmother dying alone, and to reassure me that my grandmother knew how much I cared.

My Fear Was Healed
by Helen Kolaitis

In the summer of 1996, my son Michael had a great summer vacation, which he desperately needed after enduring three open-heart surgeries in May of that year. He was doing great, until the fall came. We went to the doctors, and in September they told me that he needed to have another operation. I was devastated and went into a depression, feeling suicidal. The doctors medicated me.

Three days later, my best girlfriend insisted that we go to a local bagel shop with Michael and her young daughter. The shop was all glass, and had only one door leading in and out of it. We found a table in the back, where my son and I were facing away from the other customers. At that moment, an elderly woman came up behind us and put her hand on Michael's right shoulder. She said, "He sits there with such great strength."

Then the woman asked my son's name. When I replied, "Michael," she said, "Of course! Michael, the archangel." I noticed that the woman had blondish-gray hair. She was wearing an old brown coat, and a gold ring with a religious symbol. She then told us to have a great day as she prepared to leave our table.

We watched her turn around, but we never saw her go out the door or exit the parking lot! It was like she just vanished into thin air! After that moment, I took no more drugs. I was happy, and had no more fear of my son dying. That December, Michael had his operation. We got through it, and all went well. I see now that the elderly lady was an angel, sent to give me strength and the will to live.

BLESS HER HEART
by Susan Sansom

In 1994, at the age of 44, I awoke at 4:30 A.M. to incredible chest pains. The pains were so severe that my husband called an ambulance. Several paramedics arrived, and they confirmed that I was having a heart attack. They shared this news with my husband, but they all decided not to tell me. En route to the hospital, I told the paramedics that I felt like I was going away, and that they sounded strange and distant. At that moment, I let go and died.

I heard the paramedics frantically saying that I had flatlined. I watched one of them, a tall blonde woman, scream, "You're not doing this to me!" as she slammed me in the chest. I saw her hit me and was somewhat surprised that I didn't feel it! I was revived and was code red at the local hospital.

I was going in and out of consciousness in the emergency room, with three doctors and several nurses in attendance. I was administered beta-blockers, and the doctors told my husband to call my family members so that they could come and say their final farewells to me. As the drugs coursed through my system, I felt cold, the deepest and most bone-chilling cold I have ever experienced.

Still uninformed about the severity and details of my condition, I started talking to a nurse. She had the sweetest smile and held my hand. She was of medium build and looked matronly. She didn't wear a regular nurse's uniform, which, in my confused state, I didn't question. She told me that I'd indeed had a heart attack, but that it was over and I would never have another one. This news greatly eased my mind, and I drifted off to sleep.

When I awoke, I was in the intensive care unit, and a doctor asked me to decide which hospital I would like to use for my heart surgery. He also stated that I was to undergo cauterization at 1 P.M. that day and that I was in a very bad way. Normally they scheduled such procedures for the following day, but as he explained, I was likely to have a fatal heart attack at any time. A helicopter would soon land on the hospital roof and transport me to a town 30 miles away for immediate surgery.

To say that I was confused by this news would be an understatement, since the nurse had assured me that I would never again have a heart attack. At 1 P.M., I went to the coronary lab and was given the cauterization. Although 40 percent of my heart was not working, the doctors were astonished that I had no blockage left and no need for surgery.

One week later, I was released. The doctor said that the damaged heart could possibly recover over time, but I would still probably suffer 15 to 20 percent permanent damage to the muscle.

Several weeks later, I returned to the hospital for a stress test and was eager to talk to the nurse who had been so reassuring. I scanned all the faces and met some of the nurses who had attended me that night. They firmly assured me that no such person had been with me that night in the room! I also learned that hospital policy would never have allowed any staff member to say such things to me, since my prognosis at that time was dire!

Fifteen months later, my heart doctor dismissed me and said that he was amazed that my heart muscle showed no damage. He said, "Whatever you've done has worked!" Since that time, I had unrelated, minor surgery and had to inform the hospital that I'd had a heart attack, which surprised them since my EKG showed no problem with my heart at all. They even asked me if I was sure!

What I *am* sure about is that the kindly nurse was my very own guardian angel!

VISIONS OF DECEASED LOVED ONES

ANGELS HELPED DAD STAY WITH US
by Dianne Galligan

Fourteen years ago, I lost my younger brother (age 29) to suicide. When I got home on the day of his funeral, my answering-machine tape had all been used up. Yet everyone who knew me would have known that I was at my brother's funeral. I played the tape, and all I heard was an electrical sound throughout the whole recording. I knew that it was my brother communicating with me. He used to call me up and tease me on my answering machine all the time.

A month later, my father had a massive heart attack. My brother appeared to me (I *know* I wasn't sleeping!) and told me he would be coming to get my dad. I begged him not to take my father because this was only a month after his own death. I told him that we needed Dad, and my mother couldn't possibly handle another loss so soon. So I prayed to God and sent angels to my father to protect him. I called the hospital, and they told me that my dad was having a very bad night.

I know it was the angels that helped Dad stay with us for another eight years even though his heart was very weak. When my father died in 1994, the doctors said they didn't know how he had lived so long because his heart was so damaged. But I knew why!

THANK YOU, DAD!
by Peggy Keating

My father died in 1973. Approximately two years later, he saved my life.

I was driving late at night, very tired. Foolishly, I was determined to keep going. I was drifting off to sleep, and suddenly I saw my father standing at the side of the road! He appeared in full form, wearing the same kind of clothing he had worn when he was alive—there was no mistaking him. When I looked in the rearview mirror, he was gone. Needless to say, I was wide-awake for the rest of the trip. Thank you, Dad!

WATCHING OVER US
by Catherine Kilian

My father, William, passed away from a massive heart attack when I was 13. We had a tight father-daughter relationship and did almost everything together. His passing was very tough on me because not only did I lose my dad, I lost my best friend.

Eight years later, I was seven months pregnant with my first child—what would have been my father's first grandchild. My husband and I had just finished setting up the nursery, and completely exhausted, we turned in early. In the early-morning hours, I needed to use the bathroom, and when I opened the door, my father was standing right at the threshold of the nursery, looking in. He turned, saw me, and smiled. Scared, I slammed the door shut. After realizing what I had seen, I opened the door again, and he was still there, smiling. He walked into the nursery and disappeared.

I know he is watching over my daughter every minute, and I know in my heart that he loves her.

❧❧

DAD ALWAYS ENCOURAGED ME
by Andrea

I was in my early 30s and trying to get into law school. Becoming a lawyer was a personal dream of mine, and my father and I always talked about it. When I first tried to gain admission to law school after receiving my bachelor's degree, I didn't do too well on the entrance exam, so I gave up. My dad wanted me to keep trying, but I didn't.

Soon after, though, my father passed away. He was only 48, and he just died too young. For Dad's sake, I decided to try applying to law school again. So I again took the Law School Admission Test (LSAT), and even though I studied hard, I still didn't do that well. But I was determined, so I applied to law school anyway, hoping that my good university grades would offset my poor showing on the exam.

A few weeks after I applied to law school, a friend called to tell me that she'd gotten accepted to my hoped-for school! I was very happy for her, but very sad for myself. Since I hadn't heard anything and she *had,* I naturally concluded that I hadn't been accepted. I cried and just wanted to give up. Everything I had worked so hard for was again going out the window. I was so upset that I just shut myself away from everyone. I couldn't believe that this had happened to me again. I was devastated.

That night—I will never forget this—I was asleep, and my room lit up with a very bright light. It was so bright that it woke me up. That's when I saw my dad in the center of the light. He told me that everything was going to be okay, and that I was going to be accepted by the law school. He said that I would definitely finish the program, and that my dreams of becoming a lawyer would come true.

I was so happy to see him! I wanted him to stay and talk to me, but he said he only came to tell me that he was okay and was watching over me and that things were going to turn out all right. I begged him not to go, to just stay and talk. He told me he had to go, and that his work with me was done, but that he would be with me always.

Two days later, I received the news that I had been accepted into law school! Just like Dad had promised, I graduated. Since then, I've passed the bar exams in two states and can practice law in both. My story may sound strange, but I know for a fact that my dad was there, and I won't ever forget it.

❧❧

A GREEN LIGHT FROM GRANDPA
by Tammy Zienka

While I was in my freshman year attending Kent State University in 1987, my Grandpa Jim suffered cardiac arrest while alone in his room at a hospital in Cleveland. When the staff found him several minutes later, they resuscitated him. Since he had gone for several minutes without air, they could only bring him back to a comatose state in which he was unable to respond to any verbal or physical stimuli. The only thing that kept him alive was a respirator. After five days, there were still no signs of life in my grandfather, not even an attempt to breathe on his own. The doctors said that he was "clinically" dead.

At this point, we had a family meeting to discuss the idea of signing a paper that would allow Grandpa Jim to be taken off of artificial life-support measures (called a DNR, or Do Not Resuscitate, order). Everyone agreed, except for my uncle, who wanted to wait a few more days in the hopes that Grandpa Jim would awaken and be as he always was. After this meeting, I drove back to school. It was pretty late at night, and there wasn't a lot of traffic on the roads. During the drive, I was feeling angry with my uncle and grieving the loss of my grandpa, the person who'd had the greatest positive impact on my life.

I came to a stop sign and was the only car at this intersection. I looked to the right of me, and on the front lawn of the house there I noticed the spirit of a priest standing next to a birdbath. He had a small frame, was about 5'5", and was wearing an old traditional robe with a hat like a bishop's. He appeared to be performing a rite. He was making the sign of the cross with his hands. The more I looked at him, the brighter he got.

Then, on the other side of the birdbath, Grandpa Jim appeared. He stood tall and dignified, the way I always knew him. He was dressed in a navy blue coat and white pants, just like he'd worn when he was in the Navy. His face was glowing, and he was at peace. I could feel him tell me that he wanted us to let him go—to sign the DNR order. I nodded to him, and he smiled at me. I turned to look at the traffic light and saw that it was green.

When I looked back, my grandfather and the priest were gone. When I got back to my dorm room, I called my mother and told her what had happened. Until this point, I hadn't understood why I had seen the priest. When I described him to my mother, she told me that Grandpa Jim had a friend who was a priest who had died ten years earlier. He matched my description. That was confirmation to her and the rest of my family that what I saw was real.

At the next family meeting, I told everyone about my vision. I assured them that Grandpa Jim was at peace and that it was time for us to let him go. I also reassured them that he was, and would always be, with us. Finally, my uncle agreed to the DNR order, and the document was signed. The following week, on Thanksgiving Day, Grandpa Jim's heart arrested, and he passed on.

For many days after his death, I saw green auras around every light. Like the traffic signal that I saw immediately after my vision, the color green means "go," and maybe that was his way of saying, "Thank you for letting me go."

∾∾

"I'm Sorry I Couldn't Wait"
by Kelly B. Norman

In 1991, I was overseas on a six-month deployment as a U.S. Marine. My father was back home, dying of leukemia, and I knew that it wouldn't be long. At every port, I would go to the phone center and call to see how he was doing.

When I called my father from Bahrain, a Gulf country, I knew from the sound of his voice that he was very weak. I asked him how he was doing, and he said he was in a lot of pain and that he didn't know how much longer he would be able to hold on. I asked him to hold on until I was home so I could be with him before he died. He told me he would try to wait for me. I had three more months to go before my deployment was over.

Some of my friends and I were on a bus heading for the USO (United Service Organization), when somehow we started talking about my father. I found it very strange, and knew that there was a reason why. I was just hoping that the reason wasn't the one I was thinking of. The next morning, about 0800, the company sergeant came into the building, and I knew instantly why he was there.

"Sgt. Norman, you need to go to the company office and see the commanding officer."

I reported to the commanding officer, and as soon as he opened his mouth, I started to cry.

Within hours, I was on a plane out of the Gulf heading back to Georgia for my father's funeral. Several days later, I saw a vision or

I had a dream while I was lying in bed. I saw my father descending from the ceiling. He said, "Son, I came to tell you that I'm sorry I couldn't wait for you to return. I love you, son. Good-bye." And then he ascended back through the ceiling and was gone. I lay there wondering whether I was dreaming or if I had actually just had a visit from my father. It seemed so real.

$\infty \infty$

HEAVENLY MATCHMAKER
by Melanie Wills

I grew up living with my grandmother most of the time. I loved that woman more than life itself. Then she started having health problems. My grandmother was a very strong woman. You never saw her cry. Well, her pain grew so severe that she cried constantly. I would sit and hold her hand and rub her back to comfort her.

I was doing this one evening in November of 1996, and she looked straight at me and cried, "Please, God, take me. I can't stand this pain anymore!" As much as I knew I would hurt if she left, I looked to God above and said, while holding her frail hand, "Please, God, take her so she won't suffer anymore." I stayed with her for a while longer and then told her I needed to get home to prepare for work the next day. She said, "Okay, baby, I love you. Please take care of your mother for me."

I somehow knew that would be the last time I would see my grandmother alive. I hugged her and told her I loved her so much, and I thanked her for everything she had ever done for me. In the middle of the night, my grandmother passed on.

In April of 1998, I met the man of my dreams, and we soon married and had a beautiful baby girl. Then, in August of 1999, I was sitting in my bedroom when the strangest feeling came over me. All of a sudden, standing before me was my grandmother. She was so beautiful, and I could tell that she was pain free. There was a glow around her, and it was as if a wind was blowing her gown. She said, "My baby, I love you." Then she started to walk away.

I said, "Wait a little bit. Please don't go yet. I want you to meet Kevin, my husband, and to see our precious little girl."

She turned back and said, "Honey, I knew Kevin a long time before you did. This is why I passed on. Can you understand what Nanny is saying, sweetheart? I passed on so that I could find Kevin for you. I searched and searched, and he is the one I wanted my baby girl to be with. You have a precious little girl. I know that. I was there." Then she said, "I love you," and turned and walked away into a bright hallway.

I started to say "I love you" back, but she was gone. I truly believe she is my angel.

∞ ∞

My Baby's Guardian Angel
by Janice

My grandfather from my dad's side passed away when I was 13, and I was so close to him. When I had my first baby at 21, he appeared to me, and I will never forget it!

I had just fed my son and had laid him back in the bassinet next to my bed. All of a sudden I felt cold, and there at the foot of my bed stood a form. I really couldn't make it out, and it scared me. I couldn't talk, move, or scream. This figure starting moving toward the bassinet, and I couldn't do anything. Then it spoke, and I realized it was my grandfather.

He told me, "Don't be afraid. I just wanted to see my great-grandson." He leaned over the bassinet and touched my baby. Then he disappeared, and I have never felt his presence again.

I immediately picked my baby up and called my mom. She reassured me that it was okay, because the same thing happened to her with *her* dad when my oldest sister was born. I *do* believe in angels, and I know that they surround me and my kids!

"I WILL ALWAYS BE WITH YOU"
by L.D.D.

In 1981, my mother passed away, and I was very upset. She was only 47 years old, and her death was completely unexpected. I was 21 at the time, and going through a divorce. My church had kicked me out because they said I had no grounds for divorce.

After my mom's funeral, I was at home, feeling very concerned about whether she was at peace and was reunited with my father, who had also passed away. No one else was home that day except for my daughter, who was in bed asleep. At that moment, I heard someone rattle the doorknob. I was going to the door when I saw my mother standing there in the clothes I had buried her in. I was shocked. She said, "I have come to let you know it is beautiful where I am. Don't worry any longer. I will always be with you."

Since then, she has talked to me and come to me at other times. My daughter has also seen her. We've been told by others that there is no such thing as life after death, or that it's evil to see and talk to a spirit . . . but we know what we have seen, felt, and heard; and we believe this to be very real and wonderful.

A WARNING FROM ABOVE
by Anonymous

When my brother and sisters and I were all young children, my father went to Houston for his job, while my mother and the four of us kids lived together in our home. One night my mother woke up to the smell of a particular fragrance: her mother's perfume.

She opened her eyes to see the form of her mother, who was saying, "Wake up—turn on the porch light!" My mom replied, "No, I'm tired," as she was half-asleep.

But her mother was insistent and emphatic: "Get up now and turn on the light!" So my mother got up, turned on the lights all around the house, and then went back to bed.

The next morning, she picked up the phone, only to discover that the line was dead. The telephone-repair technicians discovered that our phone lines had been cut, and they also found footprints under my bedroom window, so they went next door to call the police.

The technicians said that the person who had cut the phone lines really knew what he was doing, as the lines were underground. The police said that we were very lucky, because typically when phone lines are cut, the perpetrator has a much more sinister plan than just robbery. Putting on the lights must have scared him away. "Boy, were you lucky," the police told my mother. However, she knew there was a lot more than luck involved, and she silently thanked her mom.

Beautiful in the Light
by Sally M. Basso

Luraine was a friend for 50 years, and she was stricken with cancer about three years ago. She told no one about her illness until a year ago. I sent her healing audiotapes, and used hypnotherapy on her over the phone. She wasn't admitted to the hospital, but she would receive treatment there every day. I would call her daily, but sometimes after a very difficult day, she couldn't call me back. One Saturday morning I called but didn't hear from her. But this time, the reason she didn't call me was because she had passed away.

That night, I was getting ready to go to sleep when I saw a figure in a purple shroud. Then the shroud fell off the figure's head and shoulders, and there in a beautiful light I saw Luraine. She appeared youthful, looking like she had when she was about 30. She was very beautiful and healthy. Luraine wore a beautiful white velvet off-the-shoulders blouse, and she smiled with a heavenly look. I went to sleep feeling quite happy. The next day, I told her husband and daughter about the apparition, and they took joy in knowing that Luraine was no longer suffering.

When I Needed Him Most
by Kimberly Miller

About five years after my father died, I was going through a very stressful divorce. I was moving out on my own with two of my children, and I wasn't very confident. I started having horrible dreams every night. One night, instead of a nightmare, I was awakened by a feeling of someone sitting on my bed. Thinking my youngest had come to sleep with me, I looked up. I was astounded to see the silhouette of my father at the end of my bed. He didn't say anything; he just sat there.

This continued nightly for about two or three months, and I never had a nightmare after that time. The appearances quit just about the time things were starting to come together and I was becoming comfortable with myself. I realized that although my dad never said anything, he was there to comfort me when I needed him most.

Chapter 6

CHILDREN WHO HAVE SEEN ANGELS AND APPARITIONS

A GLORIOUS, HEAVENLY ANGEL MANIFESTED INTO FORM

by Natalia Kuna

I recall so vividly the evening of my baby cousin's christening. At the after-party at my grandparents' house, the adults were eating, drinking alcohol, and carrying on.

Toward the end of the night there was a lot of commotion over a rowdy relative with a known drinking problem. My uncle was starting to make a spectacle of himself, becoming verbally and physically aggressive and out of control in front of everybody, young and old. He got so unruly at one point that he struck at my grandfather's glass display cabinet in a rage. The whole case came down with a giant thud, and there were pieces of broken glass and china scattered all over the carpet.

Only eight years old, I was filled with uneasiness, as the whole event was quite frightening. I also became extremely worried about my father, as he was trying to defuse the situation and started to physically barricade my uncle from creating any more mayhem.

My father, although he had been drinking himself, took it upon himself to snatch the keys from this disorderly relative and drive him home, while my mother had to take me home by herself. As a clairsentient, I could also begin to feel my mother's nervousness and suffocating fear for her husband, which only added to my anxiety!

Once back at home, I lay in my bed feeling so vulnerable, and overwhelmed with concern for my father's welfare. I thought he might have an accident or that something terrible would happen.

At that moment, this glorious, heavenly angel manifested into form right in front of me, in the corner of my room. The angel looked and felt absolutely radiant and magical, with beautiful iridescent, shimmering rainbow hues surrounding and engulfing her. She felt so divinely feminine and protective, and her mere presence filled me with feelings of complete warmth and safety. Immediately I was soothed and comforted and just knew that my father would be all right. Sure enough, he came home completely safe and unscathed!

I feel forever blessed to have had this angel vision as a young child. From that moment onward, I have always believed in angels, and I knew for a fact that I had one watching over me! As a parent now, I am able to soothe and thrill my children with my very own angel story, and this helps them not only believe in the presence of angels, but also know that our family is safe and protected!

∞∞

OUT OF HARM'S WAY
by Anonymous

When I was five or six years old, I was awakened from my sleep to see a young man in a red choir robe with a red prayer book floating in my room. I screamed for my mother and father. The young man (I believe him to be my guardian angel) proceeded into my closet, and I ran down the hall to my mom and dad's room, where I stayed for the rest of the night.

Many years later, my mother and I were discussing the tear in the screen of my window that my brother and I used to climb in and out of. I told my mother that I always wondered how it got there. I knew my brother and I weren't responsible for it. She said that someone tried to break into our house through that window the night that I saw my guardian angel. She didn't want to tell me because she didn't want me to be afraid to sleep in my room. Now I know that my angel protected me from harm that night.

❦

ANGEL BABY
by Suzanna Lonchar

The little fat baby always gave me such adorable smiles. I was about 11 years old and often stopped by to play with him at our neighbor's house about three doors down. He was nicknamed Baby Butch, and I was taken by his charming smile and good nature. He was about nine months old—a beautiful infant with a head full of thick auburn curls.

Baby Butch's mother was desperate to go out one evening, but she couldn't find a babysitter. She asked my mother if I could babysit, but my mom said that I was too young for the responsibility.

Later that evening, I awakened from a deep sleep to see the most beautiful vision I'd ever encountered. Baby Butch was floating by the foot of my bed surrounded in clouds. This vision was so brilliant that it illuminated the room. He was wearing a crown; and it looked like he was surrounded by diamonds, rubies, and jewels sparkling like angel lights. He was gurgling, laughing, and happy. He had little wings and wore a little robe made of brilliant red velvet. It was the most magnificent sight! He resembled a picture of baby Jesus I had seen, with his tight auburn curls. The vision may have only lasted for a few seconds, but it was real, my eyes were wide open, and this was no dream. Afterward, I must have drifted back into a deep sleep.

In the early hours, I was suddenly awakened by someone hysterically banging on our front door. I jumped out of bed and rushed downstairs. It was our next-door neighbor hysterically screaming, "Baby Butch is dead! Baby Butch is dead!"

It was six o'clock in the morning, and his mother had just come home after leaving her children alone for the night. When she looked in the baby's crib, she discovered that he was dead. It appeared that he had strangled or smothered, for he had somehow twisted the bedsheets around his neck.

Baby Butch visited me that night to show me that he was now an angel. He was giving me the message to not grieve, because he was with Jesus. Since that time, I have known that death is not final, there *is* a heaven, and angels are real.

❧❧

What a Child Sees
by Pamela Weber

Jessica, my six-year-old daughter, told me that the angels come to her almost every evening when she wakes up in the middle of the night, and they sing her beautiful lullabies to put her back to sleep. One night, she said that she asked the angels where they go when they leave her room, and they asked if she would like to see.

When Jessica replied, "Yes!" the angels took her upward with them. She said that her surroundings became colored pink and purple and sparkly. She saw adult angels, kids, and baby angels there; and they were all singing beautiful songs. She said that they then brought her back to her room, and when the angels exited, they entered a bright light and went back up. She was so excited about this, and she looks forward to her meetings with them in her dreams.

I told her she was a very fortunate little girl, and that she should never let anything or anyone come between her and her angels.

∾ ∾

I SAW MY AUNT EVEN THOUGH I HADN'T MET HER OR HEARD ABOUT HER!
by Mary Anne Luppino

When I was seven years old, I had a dream that a snake bit my ankle, and it actually hurt so much that I awoke and sat up suddenly. I saw a figure in the doorway of my room who looked like my mother. I reached out for her, crying. When I did so, she slowly disappeared. In the next moment, my babysitter came in to see why I was crying. It turned out that my mother wasn't even home yet.

In later years, I realized that the spirit I saw was my mother's sister, Belle, who had died when she was 18. Belle and my mother looked almost exactly alike. Years later, a psychic who didn't know about my deceased aunt informed me that a woman named Belle was my guardian angel. She described Belle, and told me what kind of dress she was wearing. When I repeated the description to my mother, she started to cry, because that had been her sister's favorite dress.

∾ ∾

THE GRANDFATHER I'D NEVER KNOWN
by Luann Brown

When I was 16, on December 20 at 2:10 A.M., the phone rang with the news that an ambulance had just been called for my grandmother, who was very ill. My dad met her at the hospital, and they admitted her to the intensive care unit, saying she'd had a heart attack. When he left, she had been okay and able to talk to him.

My grandmother had lived with us since I was five years old, and she and I were very close. We shared many special stories throughout these years, and she was more like a second mother to me. When my dad came home, he told us all the details about Grandma's condition, and said she was resting comfortably. The next morning at 7:30, I was drying my hair in my bedroom in front of the mirror. My parents had gone to work already, and I saw a man standing in my doorway. He said, "Your grandmother has passed away." I turned around, but there was nobody there!

I was so scared that I called my father, who told me to phone the police and said that he would be right home. He worked about five minutes away, and the police were there when he got home. They searched our house and found nothing. After they left, my father drove me to school. Nobody ever asked me if the man had said anything. After school, my parents were there to pick me up, which they'd never done before. We got home, and my father then told me that my grandmother had indeed passed away.

All I said was I that I already knew. He asked me how I knew, and then I told him what the man had said. Dad began to sob. To this day, he swears it must have been his father who told me. My grandfather had passed away when my father was just 14.

THE SWIMMING~POOL ANGEL
by Jenn Krejci

I remember the day an angel saved my life like it was yesterday! I must have been about five years old. I was in my yard in Poughkeepsie, New York. Hearing laughter, I ran to the white picket fence. My neighbor friend and his mom were splashing around in their pool.

They saw me staring at them and yelled over: "Jennifer, would you like to come swimming with us?"

Of course a second later I ran into my house, asked my mom's permission, and changed into my bathing suit. I didn't know how to swim, and the safest way for me to play in the pool was with one of those doughnut-shaped inflatable inner tubes. It must have taken all of 20 seconds for me to cross the alley, open the gate to my neighbors' house, dash up the metal stairs to the pool platform, step into an inner tube, and jump in.

As the afternoon went on, lounging in the pool, I found myself wondering what would happen if I let go of the tube. Should I do it? My arms were getting tired—what if I just let go for a second? Nobody was looking. The mom's back was turned; she was in the water at the other end talking to someone standing at the pool's edge, and my little friend was inside taking a bathroom break.

So, I let go for a second and kicked my legs, and I stayed afloat . . . for about three seconds—then I went under. I couldn't grip the wet tube. I remember not panicking, but just wondering how I was supposed to stop sinking. I was holding my breath, seeing the surface of the pool getting farther and farther away. I remember how pretty the wavy sun looked from under the water, and the beautiful blue sky, too.

I hit the bottom and reached for the inner tube. It was too far away. I tried jumping up to grasp it. I couldn't. I was still holding my breath, not panicking. I knew I wasn't supposed to be underwater like this, but how would I get to the surface?

As I stretched my arms up again, someone grabbed my wrists and quickly pulled me straight up out of the water. I saw brown hair and the blue sky and thought for sure it was my friend's mom and I was in trouble for letting go of my inner tube! Up, up, up I quickly came; I was pulled straight back through the tube; and my hands were placed around its sides. It was as if I'd never let go.

I took a giant breath as I quickly wiped the hair and water from my eyes, and I looked around to thank my friend's mom . . . but her back was still turned, and she was still talking to the same person. My little friend had just come out the back door of the house. I thought, *Who was that brown-haired person who grabbed me and pulled me back up through my tube?* I never said anything, because I would surely get in trouble for letting go in the first place!

Today, as a babysitter for multiple families, I tell every child I watch about how a brown-haired angel saved me from drowning, but disappeared before I could thank her! I tell them that when an accident is avoided, you say have to say, "Thank you, angels!"

A Giver, Not a Taker
by Lee Lahoud

When I was 11 years old, my father killed himself, and my mother developed a drinking problem, rendering her emotionally unavailable to help me understand or deal with this tragedy. I had learned in Sunday School that suicide was the worst sin there was, so I was really concerned about what had happened to my father. Was he in hell? Was it somehow my fault?

The only place I knew to go for answers was our church, so I shared my concerns with my pastor. Yes, I was told, my father was definitely in hell; and what's more, I too was going to hell, as were my children, and theirs, for four generations. The sins of the father must be borne by the children, I was told. Someone must pay, and that someone was me.

I was devastated. There seemed to be no reason for me to continue to live—no hope, nothing. Why would I ever have children, knowing that they were condemned from birth? I went home, sat on the floor in my bedroom, and decided to die. Then I saw a light. At first I thought it was sunlight filling the room, but actually, there in the light, sitting cross-legged on the floor with me, was a very happy, smiling man. He had beautiful long, glowing hair. I was fascinated with his hair, and the fact that he was so happy! We had a conversation that, at the time, seemed to be the most normal and natural thing in the world.

He told me I could die if I wanted to—that it was entirely my choice. There was no judgment attached to this, no right or wrong—just consequences. Either way I chose, I really was okay. But I also knew that if I *did* decide to die, I would come back and be in that same situation, making the same decision, all over again. I was sure that I didn't want that, so I decided I would stay.

The angel then urged me to decide *how* I would live. I saw two distinct paths—that of a "giver to life" and that of a "taker from life"—and I was to choose one. Again, there was no judgment in this decision. It was completely my choice. I was shown a vision of where each path led. I considered both . . . and I chose the path of a "giver."

∽∾ ∽∾

ARIEL'S VISIT FROM GRANDPA
by Mary Ellen

When my daughter, Ariel, was eight years old, I learned that she had many spiritual gifts. Ariel could see auras, hear her guides and angels, and tell you about the integrity and intentions of people.

One night, Ariel called to me from her bedroom. In her sweet and gentle voice, she said that her grandfather was asleep in the extra bed in her room. Ariel's grandfather had died six years before. I was a little nervous about why he was there and if it "spooked" her.

So I asked Ariel what he was doing there, and she replied, "He has come to see how I have grown."

From that moment, I was at peace with her gifts. I knew that they were from God and would protect and guide her in life in a way

I never could. When a mother knows that her daughter is guided by angels, it makes child rearing a joy and not a worry.

FROM THE MOUTHS OF BABES
by Doreen Wetter

Bedtime was my two-year old daughter Brittany's least favorite time of the day. At night, she would beg us to stay with her until she fell asleep. This was very taxing on my husband and me.

One night I was all prepared for a struggle from Brittany when she said, "Mommy, you don't have to stay here until I fall asleep—the angels will tuck me in." Brittany went on to describe beautiful people in long, shiny white coats. These beautiful people sang her to sleep.

"I'LL BE HERE WAITING FOR ALL OF YOU"
by Diane Lynn Willard Zarro

I was nine years old when my grandmother died of a massive heart attack. I had just found out about her death, and I locked myself in the bathroom so I could be alone. I had never known anyone who had died before and began wondering where she had gone, what really happened to her soul, and similar concerns. I had only been to church a few times as a child, but I had a deep belief in God and talked to Him through prayer every night. So in the bathroom alone, I began praying, asking for some kind of sign that my grandmother still existed and that she wasn't alone or frightened in the dark, feeling pain.

Almost immediately, my grandmother appeared across the room, in a shimmering translucent cloud. It looked as though I were peering through an aquarium full of water. My grandmother, usually plain, looked so beautiful and happy. She was dressed in a pretty turquoise dress, and her hair was done up as if she were going out to a special event.

She spoke. She wasn't actually moving her mouth, but her voice was clearly projected into my mind. She said, "Hi, honey. I only have a little time, but I want to let you know that I'm okay. I'm here with my mother, my sister, and the rest of my family who has passed on." Tears welled up in my eyes, and I became afraid. Her image instantly started to blur, and she said, "I don't want to frighten you, so I'll go now."

I said aloud, "No, don't go. I'm sorry. I'm not afraid." *Oh God, please don't take her away yet.* "Please stay!"

As my grandmother's image disappeared, she said, "I can't stay. I only have a couple more moments with you. I really shouldn't be here now. But I wanted to be sure you knew that I'm all right. I'm happy, and I have no more pain. I'll be here waiting for all of you when it's your time, many years from now." And she was gone.

This experience helped me know that God has a direction for each of us. I'm not afraid of death for myself, and I know that when my other family members pass on, they *will* go on to a greater place.

It was a precious moment in my life, and I'll never forget it.

A CLASSROOM FULL OF ANGELS
by Janette Rodríguez

My son, Matthew, had just turned five years old and was ready for kindergarten. I was concerned about him because I knew that he was clairvoyant and clairsentient.

In our home, we'd always talked of angels and God. We shared our visions and dreams, and we would see angels in our home throughout the day. My daughter, Faith, had gone through a few situations when expressing her spirit at school that led us to believe that many people aren't willing to accept who they truly are. As a result, Faith shut down her gifts of clairvoyance and claircognizance. Children can be very cruel to one another, so Faith learned what *not* to share at school.

So, this was my concern for Matthew, because he is even more verbally expressive than his sister, which could have made him a target for ridicule. So I prayed continually about the situation.

My prayers were definitely answered! When I came to pick Matthew up from his first day of school, he ran into my arms, exclaiming, "My teacher believes in angels, Mom! And she wants to talk to you."

I met Matthew's teacher, a very pleasant woman. As we went into deeper conversation, she mentioned how wonderful it was having my son in her class, and how funny it was that she also had six other students that talked of angels so openly. She said that this had never happened before, and what a wonderful blessing it was.

Now when I take Matthew to school each morning, there is music in the classroom to create a tranquil mood—his teacher plays CDs that have "Angel" in the titles. Matthew tells me that the class even has a special chair for the angels, and they all get to have snack time together!

Soothing Baby Carly Back to Sleep
by Brenda Colling

I was babysitting at the Sydney Hilton while the mother of baby Carly attended a conference when an amazing thing happened.

It was late in the evening, and Carly was fast asleep. Everything was going well—or so I thought! Then something startled her, and she began to cry. Carly was now awake.

I crept into her room, and there she was, standing up in her porta-cot, rubbing her eyes. She looked a little stunned to see me there instead of her mother. Hoping she wouldn't be alarmed by the sight of me, I quickly called in the angels to help settle her down so her mother didn't have to come back early.

I summoned Archangel Chamuel's loving energy to help me with the situation. With that, Carly lay down, still rubbing her eyes, but in a surprisingly calm state. I softly asked, "You can see the angels, can't you?" and with that, Carly pointed behind me!

Yes, the angels were there, and she could see them. They were looking after us and soothing beautiful baby Carly back to sleep. And sleep she did, soundly through the night. Thank you, Archangel Chamuel, for your loving assistance.

✺✺

"Don't Be Sad"
by Bill Fletcher

We lost my youngest daughter, Emma, in February 1990, when her best friend called to her from across a road, and she ran out into the path of a car without looking. She was put on life support at the hospital, but it became obvious that she was not going to recover. Emma passed away in the hospital.

My eldest daughter, Elizabeth, was too grief stricken to sleep in the room she had shared with her sister, so we moved her bed into our room. Two Sundays later, she said that she had seen Emma the previous evening, and felt comfortable returning to her own bedroom.

When I asked what had happened, Elizabeth replied that Emma had stood at the side of her bed and said, "Don't be sad; I'm all right now." I asked if it was a dream, and my daughter said she had been sitting up in bed talking to her sister, so it couldn't have been.

Then Emma's best friend (who had called to her from across the road) came to me a couple of days after and excitedly said that she, too, had seen Emma. My daughter had said to her, "Don't be sad. It had to happen, and I'm all right now."

Chapter 7

VISIONS OF JESUS AND OTHER ASCENDED MASTERS

THE CROWN OF MARY
by Tia Johnson

I dreamed that I was in a museum looking at a painting of the Virgin Mary holding the baby Jesus. Out of nowhere the painting slowly moved. The Virgin smiled at me, extended her right arm, and handed me a magnificent red crown with gold trimmings and a diamond-shaped piece of gold jewelry at the top . . . and then I woke up. I was so amazed that Mother Mary had given me a gift.

A few days later I was with my brother at a Burlington Coat Factory store. He wanted to look around, and once again something amazing happened . . . I saw miniature statues of the Virgin Mary with that same crown on her head. I nearly jumped out of my skin!

I'd gone to Catholic school for a number of years and had *never* seen an image of Mary with that particular crown. I'd seen her depicted with a blue-and-white cloak over her head or a golden halo, but never this crown. Oh, was I amazed. What validation! Here I thought that it had been a gift she'd chosen for me—I didn't know that it was "her" crown she was giving me. What an honor.

❦

An Indescribable Love
by Janine Cooper

I was living in Santa Monica in a single-unit guesthouse. During the month of June, it was often foggy, so my morning ritual was to look out the window upon awakening to see if bright light was shining in.

On this particular early morning, I had a very vivid and life-changing dream. Or was it a dream? In the "dream," I sat up in bed and glanced at the window. There on the rice blind was the shroud of Jesus—just his face, about three to four feet in size. I said to myself, "Hey, that's Jesus!" And just as I did, his face came in very clear, and a bolt of white light shot out of it right at me. The light had a paralyzing effect on me! I sat in bed and looked at my hands, and they were frozen stiff. I remember that my jaw was clenched, too. It was almost as if I'd had a seizure, but the feeling was one of total bliss.

I was not afraid at all. In fact, I had never felt more loved in my life. It was as though the light was *made* of love. As the feeling of being paralyzed eased up and the light faded away, I heard a voice say, "This is just a small sample of the power of God's love." The light withdrew, and the vision of Jesus faded away.

I awoke, sat up in bed, and sobbed for about half an hour! It was as though I had received a major healing, a gift of what is available to us anytime we ask. And it is so powerful! It was by far the most amazing and meaningful experience I've had in this lifetime.

~~∞ ∞~~

NEVER ALONE
by Kimberly McCright

When I was in college, I moved in with my grandparents since they lived in the same town as the university I was attending. After several months, I still hadn't made any friends or had any dates. I was very lonely. All around me every day there were couples and groups of friends.

I grew very depressed, and one day while I was in the shower, I just broke down and cried. I became angry with God, wondering where He was, since I felt so cold and alone. I prayed to Jesus, and I begged him to come into my life and help me through this difficult time.

As I pulled back the curtain to step out of the shower, I saw an amazing sight. The mirror was completely fogged up, except for an outline of a face with long hair, a beard, and a mustache. I could also see the outline of eyes and a nose. It looked just like Jesus!

I couldn't believe my eyes and just stood there staring. I felt a wave of warmth and love and knew that I was never alone. I can't describe the healing that took place at that moment. I felt so blessed that Jesus would show himself to me in this way, to let me know that he is always here, always listening.

The fact that this happened to me, a "nobody," really made me feel special. I realized that each of us is equally important in God's eyes; we are all deserving of His love, and He never leaves us. Since then, I have never felt lonely. Very soon after that incident, I met my best friend, who introduced me to my husband.

A Saint by My Mother's Side
by Virginia E. Perry

My mother was hospitalized with leukemia, and after repeated, fruitless blood transfusions, the doctors and my sister finally decided it was her time to join Papa in heaven. Mama was afraid to die, for she thought the devil was waiting to grab her. By phone, I tried to reassure Mom that only friendly faces and Papa would be on hand to greet her on the Other Side.

I was unemployed, living in California at the time. Needless to say, I was greatly saddened that I didn't have the plane fare to be with her. I meditated on the situation, finally seeking help from my dearest guide, St. Therese. She has even appeared to me once or twice while I've helped ailing friends.

Boldly, I asked St. Therese to go to my mother since I couldn't be there. Months after Mom's death, I was talking with my sister, Ramona. She volunteered the information that a sweet little nun had kept constant vigil by Mom's side. When I asked about her, Ramona told me the color of her habit, and that her name was Sister Therese! Thank you, God and dear St. Therese. You have never failed to answer my prayers!

"Is Jesus Over Your House?"
by Sherry L. Gunderson

I had recently read Doreen's book *Angel Visions,* and I started praying that I might have a vision of my own. Nothing happened immediately, but about a week later, I had a dream that I really didn't understand at the time. In it, I was awakened from my sleep by a call from my friend Ernie.

"Hello?" I answered the phone.

"Sherry," he asked, "is Jesus over your house?" He said it with such amazement in his voice.

I was lying on my back with the phone to my ear, looking at the ceiling and shaking my head as I answered, "No, I don't see Jesus." This dream didn't make any sense to me. In fact, I took it to mean that I wasn't religious enough.

A week later as I drove home from work, a colorful glitter in the sky caught my eye. I glanced to my left and saw what looked like the face of Jesus surrounded by a yellow light. I remember peeking over my sunglasses, asking myself if the other drivers around me could see what I was seeing.

Before I knew it, it was time for me to turn right and head north, as I was just a few minutes from my house. I was surprised that a vision of Jesus was still in the clouds when I arrived. The only difference now was that he was looking up instead of straight ahead. I also noticed that he was wearing what looked like a bandana (I have been told that it was the crown of thorns). I couldn't believe what I was seeing.

My sister's friend Pete was outside near my car. I pointed to the sky and asked him, "Tell me if that is Jesus, or am I seeing things?"

Pete looked up to the vision and said, "*That* is Jesus."

I didn't relate the two events until I realized that in my dream, when my friend Ernie asked, "Sherry, is Jesus over your house?" it was supposed to prepare me for what I was about to see a week later.

∾ ∾

JESUS HEALED ME
by Debbie Graham Hoskin

I had an experience about 20 years ago when I was on the road, singing professionally seven nights a week across the country for the

Sheraton hotel chain. Because of the grueling schedule and lack of rest, I began having trouble with my voice. I was usually hoarse in the morning, but after resting my voice all day, it would return at night. After several months of this schedule, it became increasingly difficult to recover my voice each evening.

One morning I woke up and my voice was worse than ever. I was very upset at the thought of letting the band members down, not to mention the audience. I decided to pray, because I didn't know what else to do. I closed my curtains, put a Do Not Disturb sign on my door, and took the phone off the hook. I was on my knees on the floor. I said very firmly, "God, You must fix my voice. I know You are there, and I know that You hear me. I beg You to heal my voice. I will not leave this floor until You heal my voice. I believe You can heal me." I prayed intensely for about three hours.

I started to feel a presence in the room, as if someone had just walked in. I looked over at the door and saw the face of Jesus. I became paralyzed with fear. He took the fear away from me and told me telepathically, "I am love and kindness."

He and his message were so strong that I was overcome. He approached me. I felt a hand brushing across my throat, and I sensed intense heat in that area. Then I felt the presence leave. I broke out into a sweat. I was healed, and I thanked God.

The experience changed me as a person and also changed the way I perceived life. No matter what problems I experienced, I always knew that God was my friend. It took me ten years before I told anyone about that incident. I was certain that no one would believe me. I still sing and perform; however, I became driven to fulfill a higher purpose on this earth. I now work with victims of abuse.

So Much Love!
by Marsha Zaler

I had an amazing dream that I will never forget: I was all alone in this white room, wondering where I was. Out of the corner of my eye, I saw a glorious white light. When I turned to look, I saw the Sacred Heart of Jesus with his index finger pointing to his chest. He was looking down at me so lovingly that I couldn't take my eyes off of him. He was so beautiful, and the light was so full of love.

I looked up, and from the sky the words *Jesus and Mary love you* appeared. Then the phrase fell to the ground with the loudest bang I had ever heard in my entire life. The entire dream was so moving that I woke up sobbing.

Mother Mary Lifted Me Up
by Michelle Haynes

I was just about to finish college, and it seemed as if so many challenging things were going on simultaneously. I was having a difficult time letting go of college life, and was also experiencing a deep depression. If that weren't enough, many important people in my life were moving away.

The most significant loss I experienced was that of my therapist, who was moving on. I was seeing her at a university counseling center where brief therapy was the norm because most of the counselors were interns in training. I had the rare opportunity to work with her for two years on and off; however, the termination of our sessions was inevitable.

With all of the changes and losses, I was depressed to the point of considering suicide. To help relieve my feelings of despair, I decided to go on a silent retreat. I go away every so often to be by myself as a means of regrouping, and to escape the hustle and bustle of daily life.

I usually stay at a retreat center where retiring nuns live. Going there has always given me a sense of solace. To this day, I look forward to these couple of days where I don't speak to anyone. I just spend time being with myself and talking to God. It gives me great comfort.

While I was on this particular retreat, I felt peaceful even though I was experiencing depression. On the second night of my stay, something happened that in many ways was indescribable.

I had just finished journaling and reading books on spirituality, and had fallen asleep with the lights still on. All of a sudden, the lights seemed to dim. I began to hear a humming sound like a thousand bees buzzing. Then I felt myself leaving my body. Initially, I was terrified, but then started saying in my mind, *Let go, let God.* As I continued to repeat this mantra, I felt myself lift out of my physical body until I was floating in the room.

I then noticed a white flowing entity enter the room. At first, I could not make out what it was, but then I realized that it was Mother Mary. She took my hand and led me outside of the retreat center. Then somehow we were flying in the air. I remember seeing the night lights all around me. It was an incredible sight. As we were flying, she took me to a place where I began communicating with three incredible bright lights.

To this day, I have no idea what the three entities spoke to me about. I just remember being suspended in midair over what appeared to be California, of all places! The three entities formed a triangle. As each light spoke to me, the entity would become brighter while the others lessened in intensity. Whatever they said to me changed my life. I then returned with Mother Mary to my room at the retreat center and went gently back into my body. I could hear a buzzing and feel a warm tingling sensation as I did so.

I immediately rose from my bed and knew that this experience was more than just a dream. My depression broke, and things in my life started to turn around for the better. I will never forget this experience as long as I live.

THE INCREDIBLE BRIGHTNESS!
by Susan

I was a 19-year-old newly single mother living with my parents after my baby's father abandoned us. I had only been to church about ten times in my entire life. I had never read the Bible or prayed much. Then I had a life-changing dream.

In the dream, I walked from my bedroom in my parents' house into the living room. There, sitting at the dining-room table, was Jesus, along with some other men dressed in the same style of clothing. It must have been nighttime and dark in my dream, because I felt like my parents were sleeping. Jesus had this intense glow around him.

Feeling very afraid, I ran to my parents' bedroom, trying to wake them up. I was screaming, "Go away!" to Jesus and the other men. But my parents didn't wake up. It felt like I was having a nightmare. Then, for some reason, I stopped crying and went back into the living room.

Jesus got up from the table, and he walked over to me. I was no longer scared. When he got close to me, I fell to my knees. I remember how *extremely bright* he was, like an aura. His face was peaceful and beautiful. His robe was the very brightest white, with a blue stripe on it. As I remember the dream, what stands out the most was that Jesus was so intensely bright!

Then, while I was on my knees looking at him, I starting saying, "I'm so sorry," over and over. He touched me with his left hand. I didn't see him move his lips, but I somehow heard him say, "I forgive you." When I heard these words, I felt warm, peaceful, happy, and filled with love. I had feelings that cannot be felt on this earth. I remember how very, very strong this impression was. I felt like part of the brightness of Jesus, of this immense love and warmth together. Then I woke up. I couldn't figure out why I'd had this dream, but I knew how special it was, since it felt so real.

After the dream, I got a Bible and began reading it nightly. When I got to the parts about Jesus, I experienced really strong emotions, because I felt like he was my brother and close friend.

THE HEALING TRIO
by Anonymous

I saw an apparition of Archangel Raphael, Jesus, and what I believe to be my spirit guide—an old wise man from Tibet. This happened last year when my husband was in ill health.

My husband had a very high fever and a cough that was deep and full of congestion. One night was especially bad. I prayed, and asked for God and the angels to assist in the healing of my husband.

All of a sudden, Raphael, Jesus, and a spirit guide appeared in the right corner of my bedroom. Bright white lights surrounded the trio. I received instructions from the figures to place my hands on my husband's back (the lung area) and other parts of his body so that the healing would occur.

I know that one of the images was Raphael for sure, because I'd asked for him specifically, knowing all about his mission of healing from reading Doreen's books. I recognized the other image as Jesus. I am not a fan of Jesus and was disappointed that he was there. Basically, I believe that he lived; I just don't believe that he was the son of God. I asked the universe why Jesus was with Raphael and the Tibetan man. I was angry that he was present.

The answer came quickly. I was told that he had healed many people and that he had come as a result of my request for healing. Needless to say, my husband recovered directly after this vision. Additionally, I have been more at peace about Jesus since then—I have no more anger.

AN INNER OPERATION
by Cheryl Cash

I went to India to see the avatar Sathya Sai Baba. One night we left the door of our temporary residence open because of the heat. I felt Baba come into the room and bless my hands and feet. I was thrilled, thinking, *Baba's here, and he is blessing me all over. I am blissful!*

Then I awoke to find welts on my feet and hands, realizing that what I had felt were mosquitoes. I was irritated with myself for my foolish thoughts, saying within, *Oh, it's not Baba. It's the mosquitoes.* I then saw an image of Baba walking over to my bed. He shook his finger in my face and said, "No, Cheryl, I am in everything, including the mosquitoes. I am always with you!"

Within a few weeks of returning home to Arizona, I had a vivid dream of Baba. My husband, Jim, is a very aesthetic person, meaning that he focuses on how people and things look. Jim and I weren't married yet, and he didn't like the shape of my nose. It really bothered him, and he thought that if we were to marry, perhaps sometime I would get it surgically fixed. As an adolescent, I hadn't liked the shape of my nose, either. Jim's comments recharged my teenage angst about my physical appearance, and I became very self-conscious about my fat, ball-tipped nose.

I wondered what God thought of me for going along with this. I thought about Paramahansa Yogananda, and mostly, I wondered what Sai Baba thought. Was I a shallow person to get my nose fixed, to worry about keeping someone I loved by having surgery? Why was I giving this power over to someone else?

Well, in my dream, Baba came to me. He cocked his head from side to side, looking into my eyes with a childlike playfulness. Then he asked, "So, you do not like your nose?" and I shook my head. He then said, "I'll fix it. Follow me!"

He went off into a large, bright orange tent, his right hand holding a needle up in the air. I followed him, thinking, *Oh, Baba's going to operate on my nose in my sleep—just like I read about!* But as I followed him into the tent, everything disappeared, and I woke up.

So I went to the bathroom to check my nose, fully believing that Baba had changed its appearance—but he hadn't. My nose still looked the same.

However, sometime later, Jim and I were married. When I mentioned looking for a good doctor to fix my nose, Jim had not only changed his mind, but he said that he couldn't understand why my nose had ever bothered him in the first place.

◈◈

AN EMOTIONAL HEALING WITH JESUS
by Louise Ratcliffe

When I was seven years old, I had a traumatic experience at the Catholic elementary school that I attended. Learning seemed difficult for me, and as a timid child, I avoided asking my teachers questions or requesting their help. During my first spelling test, I had such little faith in my ability that I felt my only option was to cheat to pass it. So cheat I did, in a ridiculously obvious manner. Well, much to my surprise, I was discovered.

As punishment, I was taken into the school storeroom and beaten on the hands with a ruler. The nun who carried out this cruel and humiliating beating was my teacher, Sister Anthony. My memories of her, which are as clear as yesterday—as well as the shame, hurt, and humiliation—have stayed with me all these years. Some may consider this to be a small issue, but to me it was huge.

From that day on, I spent the rest of my school years looking out the window. I switched off totally to any kind of English lesson and resigned myself to the fact that I was dumb. For many years, I felt a deep resentment toward Sister Anthony. By blaming her for my shortcomings, I blocked any healing of the situation. For a long time, I was able to get away with my bad English.

But then I had to study so that I could pass a six-hour exam that would allow me to work at a real-estate agency. I found the study time extremely stressful, as I constantly fought with the voice in my head that told me I was dumb and hopeless. Finally, I went into a meditation and asked Jesus and the angels to help me overcome my lack of belief in myself.

During my meditation, I met with Jesus. I saw and felt him say that he wished to take me on a journey. Jesus took me by the hand, smiled at me, and led me back into that classroom on that fateful day in 1969.

There stood Sister Anthony in the class full of children. But this time, instead of looking cross, she walked over to me smiling, and she crouched down, looking into my eyes. Her face had lost its hardness, as I remembered it, and I felt overwhelming love and forgiveness *for* her and *from* her. It was so real!

Sister Anthony said that she was sorry for having hurt me, and that she was no longer on the earth. She told me that she loved me and that she would help me overcome my spelling problems. Sister Anthony said that all I had to do to attain her assistance was to ask.

I passed my real-estate exam and am now taking English lessons. My spelling has steadily improved. I also discovered that I am mildly dyslexic, but I know I can overcome it, thanks to Jesus introducing me to my new angel called Sister Anthony.

THE DEEPEST FEELING OF SAFETY
by Janie Daily

My mom died when I was seven and a half years old. She was a wonderful woman, who taught me more in those few years than most mothers can teach in a lifetime. After she died, my brothers and I were left to be raised by my grandmother. She didn't like girls and blatantly told me so. My life was hell, and I often thought of committing suicide.

There were times when I would hear a male voice saying my name. My grandmother frightened me so badly by telling me that it was Satan. Maybe that's what she was taught, who knows? Anyway, one night I was so sad and was crying, missing my mom and just wanting to join her in death. At that moment at the bottom of my bed, I saw a bright white light. I looked harder, and in disbelief I could make out the apparition of a man.

He spoke to me and told me that everything would be okay. I must tell you that at that moment, I felt safer than I had ever felt. I knew it was Jesus; and today, at 38, I still can feel that secure, safe feeling.

Beautiful Little Light
by Karen Noe

A few years ago, I had quite an "enlightening" experience. I was sitting on my bed when a beautiful light came toward me. At first I was frightened, but then an incredible peace came over me. The light emanated a voice! It spoke to me, saying, *"Luce, lucina. Bella luce, lucina."* I later learned that in Italian this means: "Light, little light. Beautiful little light." Since then, I have realized that it was St. Francis who came to comfort me at that time.

In my heart, I know that he has been with me ever since! He is definitely working with me in promoting peace in this world, and love for all of God's kingdom, which of course includes animals and plants. Birds and butterflies in particular have been ever-present for me. When I am driving my children across town, which is only five minutes away, birds and butterflies go right in front of my car and stay there, flapping their wings. I know it is common for birds to be flying around, but not right in front of someone's car.

On one ride across town, my youngest son counted nine birds that flew in front of us, either right by the windshield or at ground level. One such bird made me slow down, thank goodness, because

I was going much too fast. After I did so, I noticed a police officer at the end of the block. I giggled, and thanked the bird silently for preventing me from getting a ticket.

∾ ∾ ∾

Chapter 8

Dream Visitations from Deceased Loved Ones

Dad Is Still with Us
by Michelle Massip Handel

My father died suddenly of a heart attack at age 61. My mother, my brother, and I were shocked. One night after his death, I had an auditory experience where he told me to stop making such a big deal out of it. He said that he was fine, and that he didn't want me to feel so sad. I called my mother immediately, only to find out that she'd had a similar experience.

My brother was at the beach at the time, and when he returned home, he called me. He said, "I just want you to know that I was down at the beach thinking about Dad, and he's okay." Then I told him about my mother's and my own similar experiences.

The three of us continued to have dream visitations. When I woke up from one of these visits, I felt as if I had really spent time with my dad. It felt very good. Dad and I visited in my dreams the nights before my birthday for several years. I felt like it was my birthday gift from him.

One day my mother told me that she broke down crying because she couldn't fix something in the house, something my father would have taken care of. She heard him tell her to get a tool out in the garage, and he even told her specifically where it was.

I'm no longer getting visits from my father in my dreams that I remember, but I certainly talk to him and feel his presence.

      ~~~

THE LIGHT AND THE ROSE
by Cheryl Anne

In February of 1991, my mother-in-law passed away after a long battle with chronic obstructive pulmonary disease. She died a slow and painful death, and it was a very difficult period. My firstborn son, her first grandchild, was only four months old at the time of her passing. I believe that her desire to see him kept her alive those last few months.

About a week after she died, I had a "dream" where I was somehow transported to the sanctuary of the church where my mother-in-law's memorial service had been held. For a short time, maybe a minute, I was alone. Then she appeared. She was so beautiful. She looked like herself, full figured and round faced, but glowing. I had never seen her looking so healthy and vibrant.

She greeted me in her jovial way and said, "Don't worry—I'm okay. I'm not sick anymore; it's so wonderful!" She was wearing a long, flowing flowered gown. She said that she was wearing that gown because God had placed her in a garden, and that it was more beautiful there than anyone could imagine. I could actually smell the flowers as she described them. I felt total peace.

The next thing I remember, I was awakened by my husband. We both sat straight up in bed in complete shock. The hallway outside our bedroom was filled with a magnificent light. There were no lights on in the house, and it was well past midnight. Just as the light faded away, a rose that we had saved from the memorial service spun in its vase. I was so glad we had both witnessed this or I would have probably thought I was crazy!

⚭ ⚭

DAD'S REASSURANCE
by Carol W.

My father lived alone in Arizona, quite a distance from his other family members and me. My sisters and I spoke with him by phone regularly, so when we didn't hear from him for several days, we got worried. My sister called the local police and requested that they go to Dad's home. They found my father dead on his bed. Apparently he had died several days earlier.

An autopsy was never conducted, as the coroner said that Dad had died of natural causes. However, it bothered my sisters and me that we never found out what our father died of.

Over the next few months, I would wake up out of a sound sleep with the feeling of my father's presence at the end of my bed. But I was too afraid to look at my father's apparition in case he looked frighteningly decayed, like when his body was discovered by the police. I shared this fear with my sister, and she reassured me that Dad would look just like he did when he was healthy and living.

Well, my sister was right. I had a dream where she and I were putting dishes away and talking about Dad. The next thing I remember, everything turned white around me. My sister was no longer there, and my dad was sitting at my kitchen table. I remember how good he looked, and I told him so. I also told him that I loved him and missed him. I noticed that while sitting there, he wasn't smoking or drinking coffee like he always did.

I asked him what had happened. He told me that he had died of a heart attack. After that, I woke up and have been at peace about my father ever since.

⊘⊘ ⊘⊘

NEVER TRULY LOST
by Chuck Pekala

On June 1, 1998, my father passed on suddenly. He and I were very close in our own way. Dad was born in the 1920s, and his family was not the most openly loving group of people. I hadn't embraced him since I'd been a child, and I hadn't kissed him since he'd come out of quadruple-bypass surgery six years earlier. Still, we had a relationship that was comfortable for Dad, if not 100 percent fulfilling for me. And we were both well aware of how much we loved each other.

I try very hard not to overlook special days for special people in my life, and Father's Day 1998 was no exception. I had purchased cards for Dad weeks before his passing. So, when the time came for his viewing, I felt it was very important to place his cards in his hands, and I did so.

In the cards, I wrote very personal notes to my father that I haven't shared with a soul. I had to tell him that I loved him very much. I thanked him for being the best father he knew how to be, and for never making me doubt his love. I told him I was glad he got to spend some retirement years with Mom, something I had prayed to God for all my life. And I told Dad that even though I was now a man, I would still always be his one and only little boy. I knew that he was proud of me, and we had no unresolved issues. I closed the last card by telling him that I would be thinking of him on Father's Day, and that I would feel peace in knowing he was with God.

Two weeks later, the Saturday before Father's Day arrived. That night I went to bed with thoughts of my father. I had a wonderful dream in which he walked into the room and stood silently. He looked at me and at first seemed somewhat confused, and then he slowly began to smile.

I asked, "Dad, are you okay? What do you want to tell me?"

Dad continued smiling and looked into my eyes. He replied, "I want you to know I am okay, Chuck. Do not worry. It is beautiful here, and I have never been happier." (Dad didn't have an easy life.)

I woke up with an overwhelming sense of peace and security. My father was in God's care. The world was right again.

Another month passed, and my mother had a dream about my father. In it, he stood before her holding the hand of a small blond boy.

My mother said, "I love you very much, and I miss you, honey."

Dad smiled back and said, "I know."

My mother looked at him again and said, "I am a bit confused. Who is that small boy with you?"

My father replied, "I don't know, dear, but he was lost and told me he did not want to be alone, so I took his hand to keep him company."

The dream ended. My father loved children. I found this dream to be so typical of him, and I often wonder who that child was. I pray for them both. I hope that whoever lost that boy has had their own dream and knows he is well.

Perhaps reading my words will in some way comfort someone else who has lost a loved one. Actually, I don't care for the word *lost*, in this sense, since I believe that my father is still very much with me.

I Saw My Nephew
by Anonymous

My dear nephew passed away at the age of 35 after a long struggle with malignant melanoma. He lived his last months with his parents in Chile, and the only thing that I, his godmother, could do for him from my home in the United Kingdom was pray for him. I began to pray every day to his angels to be with him and to give him faith, as well as relief from his pain.

One night I dreamed that I was there with my nephew at a family gathering. Everybody was wearing white clothes, and although it was a wedding celebration, everyone was looking sad and silent. I found my nephew sitting in an armchair, looking very weak and thin. He was surrounded by a group of good friends in white robes who were very cheerful and happy to be with him and to protect him. I woke up feeling sure that I had seen his angels in my dream.

The morning after my nephew passed away, I went into a church to pray for him. As I left, a young man came walking down the street who looked exactly like him! Even his way of walking and his clothes resembled my nephew's. I had to stop and stare in amazement, so the lad smiled . . . and his smile was also like my dear nephew's. Of course it was no apparition—he was a real person—but the "coincidence" was very striking.

Pop-Pop, My Miracle Angel
by Jessica Grzybowski

As a young girl struggling in the sixth grade, I was a very disorganized student. I would come to school and think, *Oh no! I have a test today, and I didn't even study for it!* I continued this behavior every week, unable to get it together. The teachers knew that I had the ability to excel in school, and they had me take part in enrichment programs, but I just couldn't apply myself.

One early morning, I awoke to the ringing of the telephone. I just knew that something had happened to my grandfather, whom I called "Pop-Pop." Somehow, I knew he had died. And, indeed, he had.

My family immediately headed to my grandmother's house in Long Island, New York, for the wake and burial. The emotions of grief were so strong among our large family. But there was one specific moment that I remember the most.

My two younger brothers were talking with my grandmother in her bedroom. She was giving them some of Pop-Pop's World War II memorabilia as a gift to help them remember him. I was really upset because I wished I had something to keep close to my heart as well, but I didn't receive anything.

Because of the funeral, I missed over a week of school, and it was extremely difficult to catch up. As I sat in my bedroom, trying so hard to complete all my missed assignments, I started crying uncontrollably. I felt like I was pinned under something heavy, and I had no concept of how to get out. My emotional outburst lasted for probably two hours until I just couldn't cry any longer. I felt so lost!

That night I went to sleep, and I had the most amazing dream. I was at my grandmother's house with all my relatives. We were sitting in the dining room having a big dinner, as we had done so many other times before. My grandfather sat at the head of the table, and he ate his favorite food: mashed potatoes. I remember looking up at him, and then he spoke to me. He said, "I'm sorry, honey, that I don't have anything for you." I just looked up at him, and I felt like everything was okay.

After that experience, my life turned around in so many ways. Academically, I was a completely different person. It was as if the old version of me didn't even exist. I was awarded "Most Improved Student" for the year. The following two years, I became valedictorian of my seventh- and eighth-grade classes. I graduated from high school 10th in my class, out of 460 students.

I attribute my success to my Pop-Pop. His visitation was a true gift. I still have dreams of him to this day. I can feel his presence when I visit my relatives in New York. He was my angel, my guiding spirit who cleared all the fear out of my heart. Without that fear, I was able to accomplish miracles!

GRANDMA'S RED ROSE
by Susan E. Watters

It was 1972, the year I graduated from high school. My maternal grandmother had been ill for some time. She lived in another state and had wanted to see me for quite a while. We didn't have much money, and not even my mother could go that distance to visit her. My aunt, who lived with her and took care of her, said she asked to see me all the time.

My mother had two jobs and was working her second one when I came home one night with Butch, my boyfriend at the time. We were sitting on the couch, and the strangest feeling came over me. I told him that my grandmother had just died. He laughed and told me I was crazy.

Just then the phone rang. I told Butch I didn't want to answer because I knew it was my uncle saying that my grandmother was gone. Again, Butch just laughed.

I answered the phone, and it was, in fact, my uncle telling me that she had passed over. I called my mom at her job, and she came home. Mom went to my grandmother's funeral, but when she came back, she never said anything at all about it.

The night after Mom came home, I dreamed that my grandmother was walking through my bedroom door. My first thought was: *How can this be? She's dead.* She continued to walk toward me, and I was afraid. I thought that I shouldn't be, because it was just Grandma. But then I would think, *She's dead!*

She looked younger than I had ever seen her, wearing a navy blue dress with big white polka dots, and she was smiling. I sat up on the edge of my bed, and she sat beside me. It was as if we were talking, but through our minds, not our mouths. She knew I was scared and was telling me that it was okay. Grandma had a red rose in her hand that she wanted to give me, and I was afraid to take it. Again, she told me (with her mind, it seemed) that it was okay. I took the rose, she smiled, and I woke up. Or was I asleep, really? I don't think so. I believe that she visited me because she had wanted to see me. I woke up screaming, and my mom came into my room.

When I told her about the dream, she said that I was weird, and walked out crying. Then she came back into my room and told me that Grandma had indeed looked a lot younger and been buried in that very dress, and that she (my mom) had placed a red rose in her hands before they closed the casket.

Yes, I believe in the spirit world that is beyond "life." No doubt about that.

≈≈

ALL IS FORGIVEN
by Jacki Whitford

My father passed away in January of 1981 at the age of 56 from alcohol abuse. We stayed with him over the weekend, but on the day of his death, he told us all to go to work. It was a Monday, and he didn't want us to miss work on his account. I called frequently that day, up until about 8 P.M. He passed away at 10 P.M. I was devastated that I didn't have a chance to say good-bye and a final "I love you."

Ten years later, I dreamed that I was standing on the street of my childhood home, next to the mailbox. I turned and looked through the night mist, waiting to see who was coming toward me. It was my father, looking like a healthy 30-something man.

He said nothing, but just pulled me into his arms and held me. I felt an intense rush of bliss. Every fight we'd ever had, every negative thought and emotion, every trauma that had ever occurred between us . . . disintegrated into pure love. I heard someone sobbing, and realized I had awoken with a start. I felt as if I had been shoved back into my body. I no longer had issues with my father; I had a sense of closure. I also had a sense of what it's like in heaven: pure bliss, pure love, pure rapture.

≈≈

A Divine Message from Dad
by Judith Waite

My father, Colin, died in 1987 from a heart attack and also hardening of the arteries. This condition was caused by his two vices: drinking beer and smoking. He would say these two habits "never hurt anyone" but himself . . . how untrue. When someone dies unexpectedly, the family is devastated.

My father was not a religious or spiritual man, and I only knew of him going to church at funerals, weddings, and baptisms. But he came to me in dream form several times and was much more spiritually knowledgeable than he had appeared when in earthly form. He spoke to me about his being there to help Mom and also to help me with personal problems. When I woke up, I could still feel the warmth of his hand holding mine.

Sometime later, I heard my father speak to me. I was astounded by how spiritually wise he was. He said, "There is no 'early,' mistimed death. It is all worked to plan—not God's plan, as such—but each individual as they come to earthly life also chooses their time of departure. No baby is born without this understanding.

"We come to give; then we leave. I have helped out many since I have been in this state, and I continue because I love this work. I have never been at my grave site for very long. The grave is a repository for bones and ashes, but not spirit. We 'honor the dead' by 'visiting' them at a grave . . . hogwash! I am more alive than I ever was in body. If you believe death to be a sentence with a full stop at the end, that's okay, but the pain is in the suffering of those left behind. If we can move on, however, the suffering will ease, and many more can learn that Spirit is always there to help."

WARM, LOVING ENERGY
by Laura Riffel

I had been very close to a lady for quite some time. One day my daughter was babysitting her children and had some problems with one of her sons. I happened to be next door, so I stopped by to say hello. While I was there, I talked to the boy who was misbehaving. Later, when my friend heard that I'd talked to her son about his behavior, she became very angry. She thought my daughter had specifically called me over to lecture him. My friend then yelled at my daughter, which led to an argument between the two of us. After that, we stopped talking to each other.

Then at the age of 29, my friend died very suddenly. I felt horrible about our unresolved fight. I fretted about it frequently. About two weeks after she passed on, I had a very vivid dream "encounter" with my friend.

In the dream, we were talking face-to-face in a very sunny and beautiful place. We discussed our fight and agreed that it was silly, and that we were both just protecting our children. She said it didn't matter, that everything was beautiful, and that I should forget about it, as she was not upset and I shouldn't be either. Then she giggled, and I felt fluttering wings all over my back and saw a brilliant light.

At that moment, I awoke and was burning up with heat. My husband woke up at that exact moment for the same reason. We checked the thermostat, and it was turned down. I feel that the heat came from the extreme energy of my angelic visit. I truly believe that my friend visited me to ease my suffering over our fight.

"Eat Fish!"
by Lynn Geosits

In 1987, my favorite uncle, Lou Garrett, passed away. About six months later, Uncle Lou appeared to me in the dream state. He stood next to a woman who was dressed as a nurse. "Eat fish!" he told me. Then he disappeared.

I felt energized by his visit, yet I had so many things I wanted to talk to him about that I was disappointed he was gone and had only told me to eat fish! I had been a vegetarian for almost 20 years, and his message was difficult for me to hear. It took me a year to add fish to my diet, but eventually I did so. I was living on the West Coast at the time, and I came to enjoy the fresh fish. Then I moved inland and disregarded his message again.

Soon afterward, I developed a tremor in my nervous system and head. The neurologist said I would have it the rest of my life and that there was no cure. Frustrated with her dismal diagnosis, I contacted a medical intuitive. She said I was suffering from malnutrition and needed more protein. She explained that I had overdone the soy and beans, and my body needed other sources of protein and iodine.

I immediately remembered the visitation by my uncle and realized that he was guiding me about this even before I had gotten sick. I followed the intuitive's advice and added fish back into my diet. Now, the tremor is totally gone! If I had been more diligent in following my uncle's guidance, I probably wouldn't have gotten the condition in the first place. I know that Uncle Lou was my angel that day and saw what I needed! Incidentally, in real life he had been a chiropractor and had been very interested in new healing techniques.

She Touched Us
by Jennifer Aldrich

My mother passed away about three years ago. She was a huge believer in angels. I did not start to believe in them until she got cancer and was dying. A few months after she passed on, I began having dreams with her in them, and each time my sister would have a similar dream within a couple of days, before or after mine.

One dream in particular touched both my husband and me. I had this dream right after we bought our first house and moved in. In the dream, we were settling into bed, and across from us was a piano. I had just fallen asleep and was awakened by the piano playing music, and a white foggy light.

The light "stood up" and came over the bed. I saw my mom's face, and she just smiled very big at me. Then she reached out and touched my hand and my husband's. I woke up right after that. I had really felt her touch, and I was crying. When I told my husband about the dream, he said that he, too, had felt my mother touch his hand.

She has not been back since. I do miss her greatly, but I know she is home in heaven where she wanted to be.

❧❧

Extra Time with Dad
by Tatia Manahan-Heine

In January of 2001, I was married for the first time. Eleven days later, my father was found dead. I was horrified to hear the news, since Dad had seemed fine at the wedding. I later found out that when I had walked down the aisle, he turned to friends in the audience and said, "My job is now done here." It was as if he knew he was going to die less than two weeks later.

Traveling to my parents' home, I cried the whole way on the plane. I cried so hard that my body shook. Since my dad didn't talk much about religion or spirituality, I was unsure how he was doing in heaven. I asked God three specific questions:

1. "Is Dad with You?"
2. "What time did he die?" (The coroner determined that he died sometime on Tuesday, but he wasn't discovered until Wednesday.)
3. "Is he happy where he is?"

I received my answer in Dad's poignant way when I arrived at my parents' house.

My dad had worked for Columbia Gas in Ohio, and had known a lot about heating systems. So I could tell that Dad was making his presence known when the heat went out in the house. A repair technician said that a heating switch had been turned off, yet nobody had been in the house, and it's unlikely that anyone but Dad would have known about this particular switch.

I wanted to feel close to Dad, so I took some blankets and told my mother that I was going to sleep in Dad's bedroom while she and my sister slept downstairs. But as soon as I said that, the lights blew out. I guess Dad didn't want me to sleep there for some reason!

So, I went to bed in another room, and Dad came to me in an extremely vivid dream. I just knew that it was him—*I saw him!* He was glowing. Dad told me that he was okay and not to worry anymore. He said that he was with my mom's side of the family. Her two deceased brothers then greeted him, and he repeated that I shouldn't worry. And then, as if in answer to my question to God about the time of his death, I saw Dad walking; he looked at a clock and started to fall, and the clock said 8:42 P.M. After that everything went black, so I took this to mean that this was the time he'd made his transition to the Other Side.

The next day, I was able to tell the funeral director what my father had been wearing. And when he handed us Dad's clothing and belongings, I wasn't surprised to find the exact outfit I had seen Dad wearing in my dream visitation.

Dad must have been visiting the whole family and neighbors, too, because nobody knew of my dreams, yet they started mentioning that they'd seen him the night before in *their* dreams. At first, my mom—who hadn't seen Dad in a dream—didn't believe me, until I described her two brothers whom I saw with him in the afterlife plane. There was no other way I could have known that information.

I feel so blessed to have had the opportunity to spend a little extra time with my dad. When I miss him, I ask for a sign; and within minutes, Dad's favorite song plays on the radio to let me know he's with me.

∾ ∾

HE HELD ON TO MY SISTER
by Teresa

My sister was struck by a car on December 1, 1999. She was hit from behind and flew up on the driver's car before landing on the ground. After extensive testing, the doctor informed us that she was physically okay but had sustained a traumatic brain injury. She was thought to be in danger of losing her life, and he was unable to provide us with any answers regarding her prognosis or the effects of the injury. He said that this type of injury was usually "lethal."

Everyone we knew began praying for her recovery, which I know helped her get through the ordeal. She was taken off the ventilator the next day and was able to speak to and recognize everyone. She remained in the hospital for one week and was sent to a rehab facility to work on the few deficits (left-side weakness and difficulty concentrating) she had remaining. She was released from the rehab hospital on December 30, 1999, three weeks earlier than originally planned.

One other miracle occurred, besides the fact that everyone's prayers assisted her in healing. The weekend before the accident, my sister had told me about a dream she'd had about our brother, who'd passed away in December of 1998. She said that the dream upset her to the point that she woke up crying. In it, my brother was in an airplane, which was odd because he never flew. He was also holding an infant.

Suddenly, the airplane started to crash. Throughout, my brother continued to hold the infant tight to him. In the end, everyone in the airplane died, except for my brother and the infant.

At the time, we did not understand what this meant, but I believe we do now. My sister is 12 years younger than my brother (he was 40 when he passed away). She is the baby of the family, and to him, she was still his baby sister. I truly do believe that my brother was her guardian angel the day she was hit by the car, and he was protecting her from as much bodily injury as possible by holding her in his arms. I have always believed that we all have guardian angels who help protect us, but I feel that my sister is a living testament to the fact that they do exist.

THE END OF THE NIGHTMARES
by Charlton Archard

It was August 1978, just before school was about to start. My three brothers, my two sisters, and I had all received new bicycles that summer. We'd all ridden our bikes to our annual dentist appointment. My sister Elizabeth was first to be in and out of the dreaded chair. She rode up the street to my stepfather's law firm to see him, but he was busy with a client, so she decided to head home alone. That was the last time we would see her alive.

Elizabeth was accosted one mile from home, driven to a dump in the woods, raped, and murdered. The man responsible for her death was tracked down, tried, and sentenced to 18 years to life in prison. Needless to say, my family struggled with the devastation of this crisis. I was 12 at the time, and the youngest in the family.

I began having recurring nightmares, but one night, Elizabeth visited me in my dreams. At first, the dream started out like so many others: I was alone at home, it was dark, and I was terrified. I was sitting on my bed when I heard footsteps in the house. I immediately went to the closet, got in, and closed the door. I could hear the footsteps growing louder and closer. I could see this person coming to kill me. The person entered my room and walked right up to the closet door. After what seemed like an eternity, the door slid slowly open. Elizabeth stood in front of me, hands held out. She said, "It's okay, Charlton, you can come out now."

The nightmares ended after that. I have kept my sister Elizabeth close to me all these years, and I've just named my baby girl after her.

$\infty \infty$

A MESSAGE FROM THE OTHER SIDE
by Christine Lamberth

My husband and I were going through a very trying time in our relationship, so on one particular night, I prayed like never before for help.

When I fell asleep, I dreamed that I was on a beach with a man in a wetsuit. I wanted to talk with him, but there was a fence separating us. I told him that I wanted to cross over and did not know how. He said that all I had to do was put out the thought, and trust. So I did, and I was lifted to the other side. Once I was standing before him, I proceeded to explain who I was. He patiently listened to me, before telling me he knew who I was and that I was pregnant.

While on the other side of the fence, I requested that he help my husband; however, he told me he could not interfere. He said that my husband was learning lessons and was on his own path. With that final message, I woke up, and shared this dream with my husband, who informed me that his father had died 15 years ago while diving with him in the ocean.

It turned out I really was pregnant at the time—just like my husband's father had told me in the dream. I had a little boy, and we named him Christopher. This dream has given me faith in angels as our guardians.

"Don't Try to Explain It"
by Tracy Cockerton

I had a dream about being at a festival or ceremony in Burma. My mother-in-law's grandmother was there. She was a small, dark, elegant Burmese lady in ceremonial dress. I had been watching the festivities, when she came up to me and gave me a Buddhist blessing.

There was someone, a Western woman, sitting farther down from me asking no one in particular what they were doing, in an ignorant kind of way. Grandmother Nat-thamé (a high Buddhist rank she attained) took my face in her hands and said to me, "Don't try to explain it to them; they won't understand."

She poured so much love on me that I didn't want her to go when the dream ended soon after. I said, "I love you; don't go!"

I woke up in the morning, still with the overwhelming feeling of love that had been showered over me. Subsequently, I spoke to my mother-in-law, and she confirmed the description of her grandmother, whom I had never met in life. She also told me that she had been praying to her, asking her to look after me.

The meaning of Grandmother Nat-thamé's message was clear. I have been learning Reiki, feng shui, and pranic healing in the last few years, something my parents don't understand. I had been trying to explain the importance of these new interests to them, telling them that they were not just hocus-pocus, airy-fairy pursuits, but I couldn't convince them. *Don't try,* Grandmother had said. To date, I have not said a thing, and my parents haven't asked. Maybe one day they will understand.

Chapter 9

DREAMS, MEDITATIONS, AND NEAR-DEATH EXPERIENCES INVOLVING ANGELS

MESSAGES FROM ARCHANGEL GABRIEL
by Tia Johnson

Two and a half years after my grandmother passed away, my mom received a phone call from the aunt of a family friend (my grandmother had been his best friend), saying that he was in the hospital. Somehow I "heard" the word *cancer*. (My mom later confirmed that he did indeed have cancer.)

About a week later, I remember being seated on the subway, waiting to get off at the last stop, when I heard a loud and clear voice: "You don't have much time to go and see him. In fact, you're already late. He doesn't have long, so you need to go and see him if you want to do so before he leaves this earth."

That's when I asked, in a semi-trance state, "Who is telling me this?"

"This is Archangel Gabriel, the messenger," was the kind reply. "I bring you news."

Roughly a week later I received another message from Gabriel: "Too late—he's gone. But he doesn't blame you, so don't feel bad for not seeing him. He knew that you wanted to come but couldn't. Don't beat yourself up about it. He is safe. He is being debriefed on his life, and is spending time with your grandmother and grandfather. He is at peace."

Two weeks after that, my mom received the news that the friend had indeed passed and that his body had been cremated. I was shocked to hear confirmation of his death, and I never again questioned what the "voices" told me.

∾ ∾

THE BIG BLUE ANGEL OF PEACE AND LOVE
by H. Titus

It has been almost seven years since the passing of my beloved grandmother. I grew up with her; she was my other mother. So many days, I remember running across the field to her house just to help her make cookies or to watch the game show *Classic Concentration* with her on the little black-and-white countertop TV set.

I would always go to Grandma's house with the excuse of wanting to dust for the quarter she gave me. We both knew that the real reason was that we loved each other's company.

I clearly remember the day of her funeral, and like a movie in my mind, I still see myself as the last one standing there at her grave after everyone left. Numb with grief, I had no tears to cry, no feeling anywhere. That day, and the feeling of being alone, has always haunted me.

Sometime later, I was feeling especially lonely and desolate. I took the day off of work and drove to the small graveyard in the small town in the countryside where my grandmother was buried. When I got there, I sat next to the headstone and cried for the first time since her death. I admitted that I was angry with God. Why did someone I love have to die of such awful cancer? Why were children hurt? What did she do to deserve this? What did *I* do to deserve this? But no answers came, and I left the cemetery feeling just as alone as I'd felt days before.

That night, I had a very powerful dream: With my back to the headstone and my head bent, crying to God, I could see a big blue beautiful angel over my left shoulder, watching me from above the headstone. I knew upon waking that my grandma was in a better place, and that all was as it should be, even if I did not understand why. That dream, although simple, left me with a great feeling of peace and love.

DREAMS OF HEALING GUIDANCE
by Sandara Smith

I was in Santa Fe, attending a class about massage therapy and spirituality. That night I got a strong urge to call my mother and check on my father. When Mom got on the phone, she told me that Dad was ill, and that she was taking him to a cancer clinic in Temple, Texas, within the next few days. I am still amazed that I called home at that time, but I feel the spiritual work I had been doing in my class opened me up to my angels' guidance.

The next evening, I returned home to Arizona, and I had my first dream encounter with angels. The two angels in my dream were very tall. They were white, with gold light emanating from their wings and bodies. I got the impression that they were very strong male angels. I only recall the face of one of them, and it was dimmed by the shine of the gold light coming off him.

Many weeks later, in another dream, the same two angels told me I needed to fly to Dad's hospital in Temple, Texas, in the morning. The words I heard didn't actually come from their lips, as much as I had a "knowing" as to what they were communicating.

Nothing like this had ever happened to me before. I wasn't even sure why I was leaving in the morning, and neither was my husband. I contacted someone to watch my children, and then I was off. When I arrived at the hospital, I found my mother on a pay phone making a call to tell me that my father had brain cancer and they were to operate in the next few days. She would have been all alone if I hadn't flown in.

My father had the surgery, and it was worse than we had anticipated. The doctors said he wouldn't survive much more than two to four months. That night the angels came again. This time, they asked me move with my children from Arizona to Dad's home in Oklahoma for the summer. The doctors hadn't even mentioned the next steps they would like to take, and the thought of a long hot summer in Oklahoma was anything but pleasant. Plus, I had been abused by this man as a child, and I wasn't really sure that I wanted to give him the loving support I felt I had missed out on.

The next morning, the doctors informed us that we had two options: take Dad home and let him die within two months, or put him in a nursing home and do chemo and hope for four months. I knew what my answer was, so I told my mom, "See you in Oklahoma. I'll get my children and fly there and set the house up."

The following months were like spending time in a personal group-therapy program. I spent hours releasing past ills by asking Dad questions about his earlier behavior. I would never have gotten the answers and the healing that accompanied them had I not followed the angels' guidance.

Toward the end of the two months, my husband and I decided to go on a vacation with our children. We headed to the beach for a wonderful and much-needed rest. However, one night during our vacation, the angels came to me in my dreams again. They told me I needed to go back to Oklahoma in the morning. When I called my mom to let her know I would be coming, she told me that Dad had gone into a coma that night.

I arrived in Oklahoma the next day. That night, for the first time in the entire two months I had been in Oklahoma, my sister, my mother, and I were all together. All at once, the room seemed to change. A feeling of great energy filled the area around us, and Dad passed on.

I can't tell you why I followed the angels' guidance. Until that time, I never remember hearing from them. The gift I received from them was priceless, though. I picked up pieces of a soul that I desperately needed. I reconnected with a man whom I had been very angry with for a long time. Now I think of him with great love and affection and find that I even thank him for the childhood I had. I was helped by God and the angels to learn what an important person I was, and that my challenging beginnings made me the loving individual I am today.

∽∽ ∽∽

The Golden Cord
by Gerborg Frick

Three years ago, I participated in a workshop and was eventually initiated as a Reiki master. During the final ceremony, we were encouraged to meditate and contemplate our individual Reiki guardian. An angel appeared to me with shoulder-length blond hair, wearing a flowing garment with a golden cord around the waist. I could not distinguish the face or gender. The angel was very tall, at least seven feet.

At the end of the meditation hour, everyone was asked to share their experience. Heather from Pennsylvania spoke first, and she described "my" angel in detail, saying, "The angel had a golden sash around the middle." At this point I was thinking, *No, it's not a sash; it's a cord,* and Heather instantly corrected herself and said, "Actually, it was a golden cord."

The group asked about the wings. We both gave our impression of the angels' wings, with the conclusion that they had nothing to do with feathers or flying, but were emanations of arched energy flowing in pastel rainbow colors. The astounding thing was that we both seemed to have encountered the same type of angel!

My Reunion with Dad
by Shirley Finch

My father lived in Idaho, and I lived in California. Dad called me late one night in April of 1979. He was crying, and he pleaded with me to come visit him and bring my two little girls before it was too late.

I said, "Oh, Dad, I'll be there in June when the girls get out of school."

He said, "It will be too late."

I talked with my dad for a while, and he kept on begging me to come. I asked if he was sick, and he said he wasn't, but he just knew that it would be too late.

One month later, my sister called me with the terrible news of Dad's death. My father passed away in a horrific auto accident while hunting with my two older brothers. I was stunned, and my phone conversation with Dad kept replaying in my mind. I was sick about it, and I chastised myself for not going.

My mother told me that, prior to the accident, Dad had been getting his things in order because he knew it was his "time." My mother thought he was crazy to say such a thing. My brothers said that the night before the accident, Dad had told them, "If I go tonight, I just want you to know how much I love you." Hours later, he was dead.

In June of 1986, I was shot with a .38 semiautomatic weapon. The bullet went through my left arm, through my lung, and then lodged in my spine. I "died" in the ambulance. The paramedics gave me CPR and a shot of adrenaline through the heart.

While I was "gone," I was traveling in this very dark space. I'm not sure if I was traveling up, down, sideways, or where. There was a little light. The closer I got, the bigger the light got. When I reached it, my dad was standing there. I was in the dark, getting ready to walk toward him because I was so happy to see him. I missed him so much! Then he said, "You're not supposed to be here now."

I said, "That's okay. I'm happy to see you." I wanted so badly to go to him and give him a hug, but my feet wouldn't budge. I could not step into the light.

In a stern voice, my dad said, "No! Go home. Your kids need you." At that moment, I opened my eyes, and my mother was in the emergency room holding my hand.

These experiences have changed me forever. Now, I live every day as if it were my last. I still make plans and have goals to look forward to, but I make an extra effort to be nice to everybody. I tell my family and friends that I love them and that I always will. And I help strangers in need. I have developed a caring heart, thanks to my experiences.

THE DAY I CHOSE TO LIVE
by Maryne Hachey

I was 16, and like most girls that age, I was on top of my game, leaving my ego to rule my world. I was moping around the house when my best friend called me and asked if I wanted to go for a drive to pick up her boyfriend's friend; enthusiastically, I agreed. A short time later, I arrived at her house, where we teased and back-combed our hair and dressed in long pencil skirts and jean jackets. Her much older boyfriend picked us up in his Audi, with a bottle of apricot brandy.

With music blaring and the sweet nectar clouding my mind, I began losing my inhibitions. This was against everything I had ever stood for, yet here I was in a car with someone who was driving under the influence. My stomach churned as an uneasiness warned me that this was not in my best interests . . . I couldn't shake the feeling that something bad was going to happen.

We finally arrived at our destination and started packing the friend's gear into the car. Seeing the state we were all in, he insisted on driving. In that moment, relief washed over me. As I grabbed the brandy and raised the bottle to my lips, taking in a big swallow, the uneasy feeling returned. This time I assumed it was the company of the boy we'd picked up.

I remember glancing down at my watch and panicking that it was already 10 o'clock and I was nowhere near the city limits, certain I was going to miss my 10:30 curfew. My friend was now in the backseat, making out with her boyfriend. Feeling the ill effects of the warmth coming from the heater, I removed my jacket, for fear I was going to throw up. I turned sideways, resting my head on my seat, forgetting to replace the seat belt I had removed.

My last conscious thought was of watching the heavy snowflakes fall against the windshield, making it impossible to see the highway. My body relaxed as I allowed sleep to take over. . . .

"Is she dead?" a voice called out above me, yet I couldn't respond.

Fear gripped my soul as I tried to moved but couldn't. "I'm here; I'm alive!" I cried out, unsure if this was a bad dream or my current reality.

Once again I was gone; my next memory was of pain coursing through my 92-pound frame as a man stood over me asking me my name, over and over. I answered him. *Can't he understand English?* I thought in my sarcastic teenage mind.

Blackness filled my awareness as I drifted through time, meeting people who weren't there. Although they talked to me meaningfully, I couldn't quite hear what they were saying.

Then the pain returned. When I opened my eyes, a man in blue scrubs explained that they were going to put me in "traction." I remember being strapped down, feeling the screw being placed through my knee for stabilization.

This time I was surrounded by white light and filled with a sense of peace as I watched everyone from slightly above my body. I was finally warm and had no pain. Beside me was a man who introduced himself as Dr. Ray. He had blue eyes and curly black hair. He seemed to be floating with me. I was comforted by his presence.

I watched as they worked frantically to revive my lifeless body. Dr. Ray turned to me and said, "You're a lucky little girl; you have many people who love you here." I looked at him wonderingly as he continued: "What would you like to do?"

His question threw me back into reality as my soul cried out, *Oh God, please don't let me die!* In that moment I felt my body hit the table hard as the pain once again returned.

I opened my eyes and looked around for Dr. Ray, but he was gone. I repeatedly asked for him, but I was told he had never been there. The date was March 31, 1989, and I was forever changed.

I later learned that I had crushed my right hip, broken my pelvis in three places, broken my right femur, and sustained a skull fracture. Due to the stress of the accident, my heart had stopped three times. I spent ten days in the ICU, but I eventually recovered. I'm sure the angels saved my life.

Thank you, Dr. Ray, my guardian angel!

∞ ∞

Gentle Beings of Light
by Dorothy Womack

As my mother lay dying, she said that her room was filled with glowing beings. They were all smiling warmly, softly touching her skin, and beckoning her to go with them. She was lifted up; and found herself walking in a beautiful, lush expanse of greenery. The place had fountains, flowers, and more glowing beings. The gardens were illuminated, but without sunlight. She wondered how she was able to walk, since she had been bedridden for four years.

These beings flew around her and lifted her up again, and she felt weightless. They brought her back to her bed, kissed her cheek, and told her she'd be coming home soon. My mother said the glowing beings were so gentle and tender. Their eyes were large and filled with love, and their bodies were small and childlike. They had wings that felt like silk and shimmered like satin. They spoke to her in whispers and encouraged her to anticipate their imminent return.

Mom said that no one should ever be afraid to die, and that we go to a beautiful place when we leave our bodies behind. Six weeks later, Mom died. Her courage in the face of certain death gave me the courage to face an uncertain life.

∾ ∾

AUNT NINA
by Sonia Huston

When I was 16, I died. It was the worst car accident in the history of the city of Vacaville, California. A police officer traveling at 65 miles per hour in a 30-mile-per-hour zone ran into the car I was riding in. She didn't have emergency lights or a siren on, as she was responding to a silent burglar alarm across town. The exact moment she came over a steep hill, my three friends and I were making a U-turn at the crest of the hill. Right in the middle of our turn, she smashed into the back and the passenger side of the car. I was sitting in the passenger seat. My two friends in the back of the car tragically died.

My injuries were severe and indeed quite life threatening. I lay in a coma and was on life support. The doctors told my family to expect the worst—that I probably wouldn't make it through the night.

While I was in the coma, my favorite aunt, who had passed away six months prior to the accident, came to me. She didn't say much, but she stood there with me while I took in the situation. Every time I turned to ask her something or cry to her, she merely smiled and nodded. I remember a glow around her, and the absolute peace that she brought to me during my state of panic. I wanted so badly to escape the confusion that filled me at that point. My first instinct was to reach out and grab her hand and go off to wherever she had come from. She just smiled, extended her hand to me, and nodded.

Then I was awake, beginning my long road to recovery. At first, the doctors assured my family that I would live as a vegetable. Then they said that I'd regain some of my old self but would never walk again. When I woke up, I couldn't speak, walk, or comprehend anything. I was an infant in a 16-year-old body. I worked through physical therapy, speech therapy, occupational therapy; and now I sit here and am writing this. I was considered dead, yet here I am promoting life.

Each time I feel that I can't go on, I go back to that moment when Aunt Nina smiled and nodded at me. Yes, the old me died then, but the me I know now was born.

∾∾ ∾∾

A Dream That Saved My Life
by Jill Wellington Schaeff

Armed with a journalism degree from Ohio State University, I was thrilled to land a job at a tiny radio station in Racine, Wisconsin, back in 1979. The hours were grueling, as I was covering evening city-council meetings, and then I was up at 3 A.M. to report the morning-drive news on the air. All this for a paltry paycheck.

After ten months of little sleep, one of the disc jockeys, Andy, asked if I'd join him in a move to a bigger station in Evansville, Indiana. Wow—a raise and a bigger market! I was really on my way at the age of 23.

Five weeks later, Andy and I were fired. The station switched to automation, and the humans became obsolete. Andy easily landed another job in Evansville, but I did not. I started to get really worried when I scouted every station in town only to find that they had no news openings. Suddenly I missed my old job, my friends, and that slim paycheck.

Andy offered to drive me back to Racine for a party weekend with the old gang. He said we could stay with his parents in nearby

Milwaukee. I called my mother in Cincinnati and told her my plans. Not a half hour later she called me back.

"Grandma is in the hospital in bad shape. I'm going to Kenosha." Amazingly, Kenosha is just ten miles south of Racine. We planned to meet for dinner and go to the hospital together. What a strange, but nice, coincidence.

A violent thunderstorm pelted Kenosha when we arrived at the restaurant. It seemed to place a heavy pall over the meal. I was thrilled to be with my mother, but I was vaguely depressed. She and Andy felt the same way, and we barely talked over dinner. But I remember that Mom asked Andy what his last name was several times.

When we arrived at the hospital, Grandma was sitting up in bed looking normal. We were confused by her spunk. She would be released the next day, and Mom wondered why she had made the long trip. I kissed her good-bye and went with Andy to attend a party with my former co-workers.

The party was a downer as well. Everyone was depressed. We couldn't put our finger on the cause of the lethargy. Andy came up to me several times to tell me that we had to leave his parents' house at 7 the next morning so he could make it back to Evansville for his first day at his new job. By 1:30 in the morning, I was exhausted.

"Let's get to my parents' house," Andy said. "We have to leave tomorrow at 7."

As I hugged everyone good-bye, various co-workers began to cry. One girl said, "Jill, we'll never see you again." That struck me as being "wrong."

"I'll visit. Don't worry. We'll get together soon," I assured them. I couldn't figure out why everyone was acting so strange.

I was relieved to collapse into bed at Andy's house. I glanced at the clock. Two in the morning. I heard a knock on my door, and Andy's mother entered. "Your mom is on the phone."

I was certain something had happened to Grandma. Andy's mother ushered me into her bedroom to use the phone. My mother was hysterical. "You can't leave with Andy tomorrow morning!" My mom had just experienced a vivid dream in bright color. A woman had come to the door and said, "Your daughter and my son were in a terrible accident. My son lived, but your daughter was killed!"

My mother sat up in bed and had a unshakable instinct to find me. She remembered Andy's last name from the conversation at dinner, grabbed a phone book, and found the number. She said she would have stood out on the highway all night to stop me from making that trip.

I went to tell Andy we couldn't leave at 7. He looked pale and shaken. He, too, had felt a horrible dread about the trip. We realized that the whole weekend had been darkened with a sense of doom.

Andy left the next morning at 8 to break any "chain" that might have been in place for an accident. My mother drove from Kenosha to pick me up and take me back to Evansville. When Andy's mother opened the door, my mom gasped. His mother was the woman in her dream!

I know angels were working overtime that weekend, and I wasn't supposed to die at the age of 23. Whenever I'm down about something, I remember God's guidance. There are no coincidences. We are never alone.

✺✺

A TRULY UNFORGETTABLE EXPERIENCE
by Nicola Kimpton

I was asleep. In my dream, I was in a big old house, lying in bed. I was trying to sleep but feeling fearful. I called out for Archangel Michael by chanting his name over and over. It was so vivid that I even "heard" myself speaking.

All of a sudden, Archangel Michael appeared in my dream! He was overhead and to my right. I had a clear vision of him. He looked youthful, with blond hair. He was smiling and emanated a powerful purple energy, which felt very reassuring. He pulled a purple cover over me as I lay in bed, and as he did so, he spoke to me, offering words of encouragement. He said that I was doing well, but that I should seek out like-minded souls. Then he seemed to cleanse my aura of fear and bathe my crown chakra with golden light.

Archangel Michael was loving and friendly, and I felt overcome, both by his power and his love. I didn't know what to say . . . I was so amazed and humbled by his appearance! I could only watch and listen, as if I wanted to take in every detail. It was a truly unforgettable experience.

As I woke up, I knew intuitively that this was the angels' way of saying, "Don't worry, everything's okay. You are loved. We are here." I am truly grateful for this experience. As a result of this dream, I have developed a personal relationship with Archangel Michael and now feel and recognize his presence. Through his dream visitation, Michael transformed my belief from hope to trust, and showed that he really *is* here for me . . . and for us all.

෨෨෨

Chapter 10

PRAYERS ANSWERED BY ANGELS

NO MORE TURBULENCE
by Brenda Colling

I was on a turbulent flight from Adelaide to Melbourne, after a busy weekend away. The plane not only jolted up and down, but also swayed from side to side.

I was feeling rather anxious, as I like to keep my feet firmly on the ground. I closed my eyes, asking Archangel Michael to protect us, visualizing his huge wings wrapped around the plane. As my eyes opened, the flight attendant was making his way down the aisle toward me. I noticed his name badge—it said MICHAEL. Instantly I knew we were safe and protected.

The captain's voice came over the intercom, announcing that he was taking the plane down 2,000 feet to avoid the turbulence. We had the smoothest flight after that, calmly cruising into Melbourne. Thank you, Archangel Michael, for looking after us on our journey home.

FROM THE HEART
by Anonymous

My angel story is short and sweet.

I was sitting in my bedroom, feeling down and depressed about my life. I was crying, and in my mind I started a conversation with the angels to ask them to help me. I also requested that they please show me a sign of their presence.

I wiped my eyes with a tissue, and as I looked at it, I saw that my tears had made a *perfect* heart shape on it. This certainly reassured me of my angels' presence, help, and everlasting love. I have kept the tissue to always remind me of this very special miracle.

A HEAVENLY JUMP-START
by Sharon

I had to go into town, but when I went out to my car, I discovered that someone had left the door open. The open door meant that the interior light was on too long, and my battery was completely dead.

We had a spare battery, but it didn't fit my car's terminals. My husband and I tried jump-starting the car with it, but we had no success. Then my husband brought his car around, and we tried jumping it from his battery. Still no luck. He increased the revs on his car, and I tried again . . . but still nothing.

Just as he was going back to his car to turn it off, I remembered the angels. I thought, *Raphael heals!* Then, in my mind, I cried out, *Raphael, heal my car!*

The car roared to life! I made it all the way into town without a hitch. What makes this story even more delightful is that I had to get into town before the bookstore closed. You see, I had just found out that they had Doreen's book *Angel Therapy* back in stock.

ॐ ॐ

INSTANT ASSISTANCE
by Joanne

My son, Rusty, was a bright and extremely happy child. He was full of energy and curiosity, and was very impulsive. One day I was busy in the kitchen, preparing a meal. Rusty was playing nearby. He was not yet two years old.

As I was cooking, I laid a steak knife on the countertop. I turned away for an instant, and Rusty grabbed it. When I turned back, he was smiling, ready to bolt with his prize, and expecting a gleeful chase. Still unsteady as a toddler, it was a tragedy in the making. Nothing I could have said or done would have stopped that little boy from completing his purpose. I fell to my knees and pleaded with God's angels for help. No words came from my mouth. I simply flashed thoughts instantaneously.

Rusty, still joyful and full of energy, dropped the knife. It happened so quickly and was so uncharacteristic of the chase games he initiated that I knew angels had been with us. I thanked the angels and God for helping me that day. I also became even more aware of all the good that surrounds my son!

ॐ ॐ

Angel in the Delivery Room
by Jacqueline Regina

I was with my daughter in the hospital while she was in labor. It was difficult to watch her endure so much pain, so I started praying really hard, asking for help and strength so that both of us could get through this. Just then, my daughter began to appear very sick and seemed to be looking at me for assistance. I didn't know what to do. I felt so helpless, so I prayed, "Dear God—help her!"

At that moment, I saw a very large angel appear by my daughter's bedside! It was so large that it practically filled up the whole room. This angel was looking down at my daughter, and then a few moments later, the baby started to come out—but the cord was wrapped around his neck! He was turning purple and black from lack of oxygen, and wasn't breathing. Somehow, the angel communicated to me that he would be all right. I felt this message very strongly.

I shall never forget the beautiful angel who saved my grandson. I am so grateful that heaven was there to help us.

The Parking-Space Angel
by Brendan Glanville

I was driving through Brisbane, Australia, and I was late to hear a friend make a political speech for the Queensland government. Then I remembered that we could ask angels to find us a parking space. Immediately upon asking, I heard a voice say, *Turn left, then left again.* This actually sent me in the wrong direction, but I decided to trust it and follow the directions.

Then I heard, *Turn around.* I did so immediately, into a driveway of a building. To my left, as if it was waiting for me, was a metered parking space. Then I realized that I'd forgotten my wallet in my haste, and I needed money for the parking meter. So I asked my angels for change, and when I opened my ashtray, I found the exact two coins that I needed for the meter. I was so excited upon walking into the meeting that I called my office and told my staff.

Returning to my car after the speech, I said to the angels, "If any human needs a parking space, this one has time left on the meter, and that person can have it for free." I got in my car, and before I even started it, a car came around the corner and waited until I pulled out of my space.

∾ ∾

PROTECTED FROM A TORNADO
by Judy Mitchell

In the spring of 1996, we were on a "tornado watch" where I lived in Allison, Arkansas. It was a hot, humid Sunday, and the sky was a greenish gray. Having recently moved to Arkansas from California, I was unfamiliar with tornadoes. I had seen an unusual thing in the sky the day before: a complete circular rainbow around the sun. I found out later that it's called a *sun dog,* and it indicates severe weather.

I was home babysitting a friend's son. My 13-year-old foster daughter was with me, as well as my twins, who were 8, and they were all playing inside the historic old house we were renting. I received a phone call from a neighbor saying that there was a large tornado on the ground moving toward our home! She said we needed to take cover. Well, there was no basement, only a bathroom on an outside wall with a large window. I knew from what I had read that this was not sufficient protection.

I told all the children to get their shoes on and get into the tub. The sky was growing darker and greener. I went outside to look, and there it was; I could hear it before I saw it. It was huge, spinning, and it was about a quarter mile from us. I ran back into the house to get to the children, and then everything went dark—all the electricity went off. The noise of the tornado approaching was so loud that it was almost unbearable. The house was actually vibrating.

I got on my knees in the tub with the children, covering them with my arms. I told them not to listen to the noise, but to listen to me. I thought, *We are going to die!* I thought about my grown daughter in California and hated to think of her being left alone if we didn't make it.

I started praying and asked for assistance: *Please make this tornado go up and over this house now.* Then I mentally affirmed, *We are protected. We are loved and protected now.* I asked my mother, who had passed on, to help us. I told myself, *We are not going to die; we are going to live.* The louder the noise, the louder I prayed. The sounds were unbelievable, and the shaking was tremendous, but then it all slowly subsided. When it seemed safe, I looked out the window and all I could see was green fog. We were alive and unhurt! It had passed.

Unfortunately, my neighbors were not so lucky. There was a total of six tornados at 7 P.M. that day in Allison. Nine people were killed, and many homes were destroyed. Part of my roof had been taken off, a brass bed had been thrown completely over our house, and the hubcaps on my car were sucked off. There were a number of houses where only the foundation still stood. Many people were in church that Sunday at that time of day, and they came home to find their houses gone. We did not have electricity or water for days, but we were alive.

A man came up to me and said he saw the tornado sitting on my house like a hat, and he was sure we were all dead. Then he said it just took off up into the air. He said it was a miracle. It *was*—we were assisted by God and the angels. Another man saw the tornado hit our house, and he, too, had been sure we had all perished.

This experience changed my life. I believe in prayer and know that you only need to ask. As for the children in the tub, I doubt if they will ever forget the experience, and they now know the power of prayer, as well as the importance of asking for protection.

LOST AND FOUND
by Bonnie Suzanne Koester

I had taken both of my daughters and their friends out to dinner to celebrate my oldest daughter's birthday. The restaurant was situated on the Houston Ship Channel and had a large lawn in between the water and the building. We had a great meal, and after dinner, the girls ran and frolicked on the lawn before we left. As soon as we got into the car, my daughter's friend exclaimed that she had lost her wallet with her driver's license in it.

The girls all got out of the car and started searching the lawn. It was very dark, so I parked so the headlights would shine on the lawn for them. It looked hopeless, like finding a needle in a haystack. As I sat in the car, I relaxed and asked my angels if they would please show me where the wallet was. I then saw a vision clearly in my mind's eye. I saw the wallet behind me, beside the backseat, near the door.

I got out of the car and opened the back door, fully expecting to see the wallet—that's how clear the vision had been. But I couldn't see it. It was pitch-black. I leaned closer, and then I saw a small glint of metal. I reached out, and it was the wallet! It was exactly where I'd envisioned it, even though I couldn't see it with my physical eyes. That was weird and really cool!

LOOK WHAT THE ANGELS DRAGGED IN!
by Carol Czerniec

A few years ago, I worked full-time, and my two children went to day care. My five-year-old son had a cat that he loved very much. She was fat and declawed, and we always kept her in the house. But occasionally, she would sneak out and hide under the juniper bushes, which were so sharp, sticky, and low to the ground that it was impossible to get her out.

One morning I had the kids in the car ready to go, and I had to run back into the house for something I forgot. Sure enough, that cat darted out and into the bushes. We were already late, and I knew from experience that it would take hours to get her out. I couldn't leave her there all day and risk something happening to her. My son would never forgive me!

I almost cried in despair, but instead I asked the angels to bring her back in. I stood there holding the door open, waiting for the angels to help me. Immediately, the cat came out from under the bushes. She was walking very strangely, stiff like a puppet, with her eyes looking wild. She ran right in the front door without hesitating, and I shut it behind her. I couldn't see the angels dragging her in, but both the cat and I knew they were there!

A COMFORTING MESSAGE
by Anonymous

It was a particularly difficult time for me. I had been divorced about eight years, my sons were off in college, and I was in graduate school. I felt isolated, lonely, and fearful. As I walked along the beach in the Cape Cod town where I lived, I tried to apply a nursing theory that I was studying to my own life. The Betty Neuman systems model states that if any one variable in a person's life is disrupted, the person is at risk of illness. An evaluation of me revealed an overweight, out-of-shape, isolated, and spiritually deprived woman.

As I thought about my status, I kept thinking of the influence that my early life was having on my current life. My dad had been a wonderful man when he was sober. When he drank, though, he became a monster, abusing my mother and frightening my three older sisters and me. Dad died when I was seven, adding to my feelings of loss, abandonment, and anger.

I couldn't help but resent the effect my father's alcoholism had on my psychological development. However, I decided that day on the beach to make changes in my life for my general well-being. I decided to go on a diet, walk more often, and return to church. We had always been devout Catholics, but after my divorce, I felt abandoned, even by God, so I had given up any religious affiliation.

The next morning, I got up early for church. I had a good, healthy breakfast and began reading a magazine with my coffee. There was an article about a medium who communicated with people who had passed on to another plane. I never doubted that there was life after death, so I was not as skeptical as many of my friends would have been about the communications she described. I sort of laughingly said out loud to the room, "If my father is around me, he has a lot of making up to do!"

I went on to Mass. During each service, there comes a time where we pray for those who have died. You can imagine my reaction when the priest said, "We pray for all who have died, especially for [he said my dad's name], for whom this Mass is being said." I felt a rush so strong that I turned around to see if someone had pushed me. There was no one close enough to have done so. I was so stunned by the mention of my father's name (even if there was another man with the same name in the area) so soon after I sent off my spoken message to him! The possibility of this being a coincidence does not exist for me. I know that my dad is able to see me and knows what's going on in my life, and that God allowed me to receive this reassuring message.

I'm now going to Overeaters Anonymous and am working with my angels daily. Dad's heavenly message and my angels are helping me transform my life from victimhood to victory!

Lucky Angel
by Laura Curran

I have always known that angels were a part of me, watching me, protecting me, ever-reliable, sweet guardians. I have been blessed by so many miracles in my life now that I look back and say, *Wow!*

One of the miracles that changed my life began on January 15, 2009. On this day I adopted a little boy dog—a six-pound apricot toy-poodle mix. He was three years old then. His coat had darker patches of brown that look like angel wings. He had no name, so my husband, Randy; my daughter, Lisa; and I called him "Lucky Angel." I felt in love with him right away—we all did.

Two weeks later Randy and Lisa took Lucky Angel for a walk. He got scared by another dog barking, the retractable leash fell, and he ran off. We live in the desert, where there are mountains, tumble-weeds, and dirt roads; as well as coyotes, snakes, and all kinds of other animals. Behind our house is the Edwards Air Force Base, with solitude and open land everywhere.

I received a call on my cell phone: my dog had run away. My heart sank. We hurried to search for him before darkness fell. This was February 2, 2009. It was cold in the evening; we had flashlights; and we were screaming, yelling, calling for him. He did not answer our calls.

I received a thought that evening: *Go visit Doreen Virtue's website and ask for help.* I did so. I asked the Angel Therapy Practitioners® for assistance. The response was overwhelming. Everyone gave me hope, love, and kindness.

The days went by; we posted flyers everywhere. We followed every lead. We did not give up. I prayed and prayed; and the angels stayed by my side, loving me and sending wonderful people.

Sixteen days later I received a e-mail from a Angel Therapy Prac-titioner by the name of Ellany. She wrote: "Absolutely I am feeling that Lucky is in the desert and not with anyone at this time. I hope I am wrong. May Creator God keep him protected, and may he be returned to you, his loving friend. God bless and keep you. Keep me posted on how things go." I still have her e-mail today.

I called Randy and said, "You need to come home right now. He is in the desert." When my husband drove up, I was ready to go. He wanted to walk behind the house to look for Lucky. I said no, we needed to drive back into the mountains where the water was. I had a vision of a small mud puddle behind Red Mountain where it had rained. So we started driving, and as we approached a puddle of water, there on the side of the road was my dog, *alive!*

I thought he was a mirage, but I called to him and he lifted his head, so I jumped out of the car as fast as I could. I picked him up, and I let out a cry of gratitude. We took him to the hospital, and his recovery was so fast!

Ever since then, my heart keeps opening up to love. My life has changed. I met Ellany—and she is a wonderful, loving, caring person. Things just keep getting better and better every day. I am deeply grateful to my angels and the Creator God for bringing me a dog who taught me how to feel *love.*

Chapter 11

LIFESAVING ANGEL VOICES

"YOU ARE SAFE . . . JUST LET GO"
by Nelly Coneway

We had a very intense experience on New Year's Eve 2009. My son and two of his friends went to a party, and I drove to pick them up at 3 A.M. I was very tired, but I asked the angels to protect and guide me.

On the way to drop off one of the boys at his house, I entered a narrow street with no lights and zero visibility. The road was empty—but then suddenly a huge SUV drove right in my path. Everything happened so quickly that I couldn't do anything, but I heard Archangel Michael's voice: "You are safe . . . just let go." At the moment when I thought that we would have a head-on collision, something grabbed the wheel out of my hands and turned it to the side so we escaped the crash.

It was unbelievable that we didn't have an accident. Even the kids in my car noticed it, saying, *"Wow,* that was close, a true miracle." Thanks to God and His mighty angels, the four of us survived.

⟆⟅

CLEAR AS DAY
by Victoria Granados

One day I was heading out for my usual early-morning hike. I said good-bye to my son, and let him know I was going to Mission Trails. As I was walking downstairs, I heard an angel say, clear as day, "Go to Lake Murray today; there will be more people there. It will be safer." I listened.

Later that night, my son called me from his father's house with panic in his voice. He wanted to know if I was okay. When I asked why, he said he'd just seen on the news that a woman had been attacked at Mission Trails around the same time I would have been there. I credit that angel voice with protecting me from danger that day.

⟆⟅

A CALM AND SOOTHING VOICE
by Verlain Lane

It was winter, and the weather in Kansas was cold and clear. I had a medical appointment at the hospital two hours from our home.

My two-year-old son sat on the passenger side of our 1986 Toyota four-wheel-drive truck. I noticed that the sky was clouding over and getting dark, even though it had been sunny just an hour earlier when we left home. Before we got to the I-70 ramp, it was like a thick curtain suddenly fell in front of us.

I was surprised that the snow was coming down so fast and thick that I couldn't see anything. I slowed down and thought about turning around and heading back home, but I kept going because I'd waited over two months for this appointment. Besides, we were almost halfway there. So I slowed down, and we crept along until we got to the on-ramp, because I felt sure it would clear off any minute. But it didn't.

Heading east on I-70, I saw cars off the road everywhere, and 18-wheelers slowed to a crawl. I had locked in my four-wheel drive, and I told my little son we'd be okay. I was coming up on an overpass bridge, and just as I hit the small drop-off seam of pavement, the Toyota skidded on the ice.

As this happened, I looked over and saw that my toddler had unfastened his seat belt! I reached out with my right hand and grabbed his wrist as I steered into the skid with my left hand. I couldn't bring the car out of the skid, and I couldn't let go of my baby son.

I heard a male voice plainly say, "Hold on to the boy, let go of the wheel, and close your eyes." I didn't stop to think about who was talking to me; I just did it.

When I opened my eyes, a man jerked open my driver's door and asked if I was okay. Our Toyota had jumped the overpass railing and skidded along the entire length of the concrete rail as if it were on a track. I assured the stranger we were fine, and he said he'd call for help. Most miraculous of all was the fact that my pickup didn't have a single dent or scratch!

The first words out of my toddler's mouth were, "Wow, Mama!" as he clapped his hands. Waiting for help, I tried to figure out who had spoken those words when the truck skidded out of control. It was the most serene, controlled, masculine voice I'd ever heard. So calm and soothing. I remember doing as I was told; and a peaceful, loving feeling wrapped around me. It was as if my son and I were being held tightly in a giant hug.

We made it to my medical appointment, and when I told the doctor (who was a golfing buddy of our family priest) what had happened, he said, "You understand you met an angel today, don't you?" I could only nod.

Although it has been 14 years, I'll never forget the loving guidance spoken to me on that icy March morning.

THANK GOD FOR THE ANGELS
by Rebecca Thrasher

I was driving home from work early, feeling overwhelmed. My youngest son, Tyler, was home sick, and I was getting married the next day. I felt totally unprepared. If that wasn't enough, I had company coming to my house for the wedding.

Tyler's doctor had said that my son had a virus, and all day long he had kept calling me to say that he felt increasingly worse. I wondered if I needed to take him to the urgent-care center. I called his doctor, who said the complaints my son was experiencing were part of his virus. I wondered, *Should I take Tyler to the medical center anyway?* I didn't want to take any chances with my son's health. But on the other hand, I had so many things to do that night, and the doctor had reassured me that Tyler's symptoms were normal.

That was when I heard a voice say, "It's his appendix!" in a loud and stern way. So I took Tyler to the clinic. The doctor began telling me that he thought it was the virus, but I said that I just wanted to be sure it wasn't his appendix. He did another exam and went to get another doctor, who did the same thing. They then sent us to the hospital to see a surgeon. Tyler had his appendix removed that night just before it burst. I thank God and His angels for saving my son's life.

KEEPING ME SAFE
by Diane Smith

One morning around 5:30 while driving to work, I was on a road where there were woods and no lights other than car headlights. All of a sudden, I heard a voice telling me to start putting my brakes on. I did, and out of the woods a large deer appeared right in front of my car.

When I started to drive again, I heard the same voice telling me not to, because there was another deer. I stopped again, and sure enough, out of the woods came another large deer.

If I hadn't listened to this voice both times, I would have hit the deer and probably injured myself, too. I know this was my guardian angel keeping me safe. This was really the first time I had heard my guardian angel, and now whenever I hear that voice, I listen.

THE ANGEL OF WHITE LIGHT
by Jim St. Onge

The weather was a mess in New England that day. Snow, sleet, freezing rain. Yuck! I was out on an errand and found the road conditions worsening as I made my way home. Up ahead in the distance, I could see two police cars and a car that had crashed into a telephone pole.

I slowed down, but my car began sliding toward the other vehicles. I quickly visualized white light surrounding my car, and I mentally yelled for the angels to bring it under control. All of a sudden, I heard a voice say, "Take your foot off the brake!"

I obeyed the instruction, and the car, which was about to lose control, slowed miraculously and stopped just before I would have crashed into a police car. As I slowly drove by the accident scene and saw the driver, I sent many angels to this woman, who seemed to be unhurt, thank God.

I give my angels much thanks for their help in this situation. They saved me from potential injury!

"SLOW DOWN!"
by Arlene Martin

I had a habit of jogging in the evenings along Lake Michigan. One night as I was running, a "voice" told me to slow my speed. I didn't listen. I started to jog a few feet, and my pedometer quit working. I stopped in order to reset it. When I returned to jogging, I again heard the voice tell me to slow down. I ignored it, and again, my pedometer stopped working. I slowed down so I could once more reset the device, and I continued my jog at a more leisurely pace.

A few minutes later, a little distance ahead, an accident occurred between two cars. One of them became airborne and landed about six yards directly in front of me, right on the jogging pathway. Had I not slowed down, I would have been hit by the car. To this day, *I know* the voice was that of my angel.

THANK GOD I LISTENED
by Debbie Hoskin

My son, Jason, had just gotten his learner's permit. It was a Sunday afternoon, and he asked if we could go driving. I thought it would be a great way to spend some quality time with him, so I agreed and let him drive. We had been driving for approximately 20 minutes down a country highway. Jason was doing a great job, so I began to relax and look at the scenery. Actually, I became very relaxed and forgot that my inexperienced 17-year-old son was at the wheel.

Suddenly something told me to stop daydreaming. It said, *Pay attention to your son driving.* Then, like a vivid daydream, I saw a flash or vision of a red car coming around the bend at us in our lane. I almost didn't pay attention to it, but I gave in to a strong feeling urging me to give instructions to my son on what to do in the event of a potential head-on collision. He listened carefully and repeated the instructions back to me.

Within a minute, a small red car came speeding around the bend of the highway, passing a slower-moving vehicle and heading toward us in our lane. My son knew exactly what to do to prevent what might have been a fatal accident. I was certain that we had been warned by a guardian angel. I expressed my gratitude many times that day and vowed to always trust my intuition.

RESCUED BY AN EARTH ANGEL
by Lorein Cipriano

I was driving on Route 8 in Connecticut after visiting a friend. It was late, around 1 o'clock in the morning. The road was very dark.

Suddenly, I saw a car parked on the side of the road. A voice said to me, "Stop! Stop!" Ordinarily, I would never stop on a dark road like this, but the voice created such an urgency in me that I slammed on the brakes and pulled over in front of the car.

I looked back and saw a woman jump out of the passenger side of the car, and she started running toward mine. The driver, a man, also got out. The woman approached the front passenger side of my car. And the voice came again: "Let her in!"

I opened the passenger door, and the woman, who was crying, got in. The man then came around my side of the car and started banging on the window. The voice said, "Go!" So I put my foot on the gas and sped away as fast as I could.

The woman told me that she'd been working late at a factory, but the person who was supposed to pick her up to take her home didn't show up, and this man (who worked in the same factory) offered her a lift.

However, on the way home, he had stopped the car and attempted to sexually molest her. She had been trying to fight him off when my car pulled over in front of them. She was grateful, to say the least, and I attribute this "rescue" to the help of her angels, and mine. I truly believe that God speaks to us and guides us through His angels.

∾ ∾

A Lifesaving Warning
by Jane Anne Morgan

Last year I was awakened by the sound of my CO_2 detector (a device that detects gas leaks) beeping. Earlier that week, my neighbor who shared the duplex had experienced a similar situation. It turned out that both of our detectors had malfunctioned within the same week.

Anyway, I was so sleepy that night that I got out of bed to unplug the detector to stop the beeping. I thought I would check on it in the morning when I was awake. Just then, though, the telephone rang. As I picked up the receiver, I heard a recorded voice say, "You have a collect call from . . ." and then a really deep and watery voice said, "You're orange," with these two words stretched out slowly.

The moment that I heard these words, I had an inner knowing: "I left my gas oven on!" When gas is dangerous, the flame burns orange. I ran to the kitchen, where I discovered that yes, I had left the oven turned on. So my detector wasn't malfunctioning; it was correctly warning me. I probably would have been dead within a couple of hours if the phone call hadn't warned me of danger.

But where did that call come from? Since it was a collect call, I waited until my phone bill arrived in the mail so I would have a record of the origination number. The bill showed that the call had come in at 4:45 A.M. from a number in Denison, Texas. I live in Oklahoma.

I called the number, and it was a place called the Cardinal Motel. The manager said there was no way to know who had placed the call that night. How would anyone there know about my gas oven? Whoever called me that night saved my life, and I believe that it was an angel.

SAVED BY MY GUARDIAN ANGEL
by Alison Clarke Taylor

I was about 20 years old and was returning to my home on a very narrow, winding country road. This road wound around trees and up over a blind hill. I always approached this hill with caution and stayed far to the right. However, there were vertical banks on both sides of the road, so there wasn't much room for two cars to pass.

That day, just as I approached this hill, I heard a voice say, "Pull over and stop." I was alone in the car. I felt the steering wheel being turned to the right, so I obeyed the voice. I sat there for about two seconds wondering why I had stopped—something I had never done in the hundreds of times I had negotiated that road.

Just as I was contemplating why I had pulled over, a woman roared over the hill in a large car, going very, very fast and completely taking up the road. I would have probably been killed or critically injured if I'd had a head-on collision with this car. I feel that my life was saved that day by my guardian angel.

The Nurse Who Talks to Angels
by Anonymous

I was working as a nurse on the night shift at Stanford Hospital in 1989. The only way for me to handle the monthly day/night rotations was to pray before I went into work, since I was sometimes there for 24 hours at a time. I prayed for Divine assistance that I could get through the night, and that I would be safe and alert for anything that arose.

One particular night while I was walking into a patient's room, I heard a voice tell me to go down to the opposite end of the hall and check on another patient of mine. I thought, *I just checked on him not too long ago, and he was sleeping and doing fine.* Normally, the nightly rounds on every patient occurred every two hours, and I had just seen that patient about 45 minutes prior.

I contemplated the voice, trying to rationalize, *But I just saw him,* yet the voice persisted. I then decided, *Okay, I'll go check on him.* I put down the other patient's medications and walked all the way down the long hallway and into this patient's room. He was sleeping, so I put my hand on his chest, asking if he was all right. As my hand touched him, I noticed something wet, so I turned on the light. I then saw that he was hemorrhaging from a central-line site where the line had been taken out during the prior shift hours before!

I immediately applied a pressure dressing. I asked the patient if he felt any pain or knew he was bleeding, and he said no. He was dreaming away! I then knew that the only way for me to have caught this hemorrhaging in the beginning was due to Divine guidance. I was very thankful, and now I really listen to my angels.

ANGEL GUIDANCE KEPT ME SAFE
by Martín W. Acevedo

One evening in March of 1997, I didn't get home until bedtime. I was very tired, and looking forward to resting. When I walked in the door, I heard a voice say in a straightforward manner: "Don't go to bed yet." The voice was neither feminine nor masculine, and it wasn't menacing or sweet. It was just calmly instructive.

I am an elder of a church that honors the spiritual beliefs of East and West, and was raised praying for the assistance of the angels, so this communiqué did not seem unusual to me. I simply said out loud, "Okay," and kept myself occupied in the living room for a while. Soon, I sensed that whatever was going to happen would happen soon. At that moment, I heard an intermittent buzzing sound coming from my kitchen.

I walked into the kitchen and saw that the electrical outlet for my refrigerator had caught on fire, and the flames were spreading up the wall! I was renting an older home at the time, and the outlet or wiring was probably worn out. I could only think, *Wow*, knowing why I had received so timely a message. I put out the fire with a small kitchen extinguisher that I kept nearby.

Thinking about the episode, I said happily to my unseen friend, "Thank you." Later, as I walked toward my bedroom, I received one more message from my guardian angel: "Check your smoke detector."

I reached up and tested the smoke detector near my bedroom and discovered that the battery was dead. Had I not been attuned to my guardian angel's message, I probably would have died from the kitchen fire, which would have gone unnoticed.

I am very grateful for the partnership that exists between heaven and Earth, so that we each can fulfill our sacred mission here. I hope this inspires others to be open to their angel friends.

An Angel Watching Over Me
by Azaya Deuel

My first angel experience happened when I was around four years old. My brothers, Bobby and Billy; my sister, Anne; and I were at a park in Azusa, California, near our home. While my siblings played with friends at one end of the park, I wandered to the fountain at the other end.

A man approached me and asked if I wanted some candy. I inquired if I could have some for my brothers and sister, too. He said yes and told me to follow him behind one of the buildings by the parking lot and he would give me all the candy I wanted. I was intent on going with him because I really wanted the candy.

As I started to follow him, though, I heard a voice say, "You have to go tell your brothers and sister where you're going." I repeated this to the man, but he tried to tell me that it wasn't necessary and that we'd only be gone a few minutes. I kept insisting that I had to tell them, and then I did as I was directed and got my brother Billy's attention. He called from across the park and asked where I was going. I told him I was going with the nice man to get some candy for all of us. I turned around to find the man gone. The other kids came running and checked the parking lot, but the man was nowhere to be found. They kept me close by after that.

Later that night, the police came to our house and asked a lot of questions. It was during a time when there were a lot of kidnappings, in late 1949. Fortunately, my angel intervened, and even more fortunately, I listened and obeyed!

"Breathe, Kate!"
by Kate Whorlow

It was 1992, a few months after my grandmother had died. I was lying in bed asleep in the early hours of the morning. I don't remember what I was dreaming about, but I think my grandmother was in my dream. Suddenly I heard someone say strongly in my right ear: "Breathe, Kate! Breathe!"

I gasped and woke up suddenly, at the same time realizing that I had actually *stopped* breathing. I immediately sat up and inhaled as deeply as I could, trying to understand what had happened. It was pretty scary, to say the least; and at first I thought my mother had come into my room, noticed that I wasn't breathing, and told me to breathe, but everyone else was still asleep and there was no one there.

Now, years later, I know that it was my angel who told me to breathe and saved my life, as I had no idea at the time that I had asthma—one symptom of which is sleep apnea (where you stop breathing in your sleep). My grandmother, I believe, sent the angel to save me, as she'd had asthma herself when she was alive.

On the Wings of Angels
by Azaya Deuel

My husband, Dan, was a pilot and flight instructor who owned his own plane. One day, Dan and I went flying from an airport in La Verne, California, and headed over the mountains of Southern California. It was an incredibly beautiful day, and everything was going well.

Suddenly, the plane's engine started to sputter and quit. Dan tried everything he could think of, but nothing helped, so he started looking for a place to crash-land. Things weren't looking too good.

I knew nothing about flying, and Dan never talked to me about airplanes or their mechanics. I actually saw my life flash before my eyes, like you read about in books.

Then I heard a voice say, "Carb heat. Tell him to pull the carb heat"—so I did. I yelled, "Carb heat! Pull on the carb heat!" I guess my outburst shocked Dan enough that he immediately pulled on the carburetor heat knob.

I'm sure all of this took place in a matter of seconds or minutes, but it seemed like an eternity. Pulling on the "carb heat" worked, and we were able to get to the airport and land safely!

As Dan explained to me later, the carburetor had iced up during storms that had occurred over the previous days, and the ice prevented the engine from receiving fuel. Once the situation was under control, my husband just looked at me and said, "How?" I told him about the angel's voice. I don't think he believed me, but I knew without a doubt that the angels were flying with our airplane that day, and that they'd just saved our lives!

THE NIGHT THE ANGELS WARNED ME OF IMPENDING DANGER
by Natalia Kuna

One late night when I was in my 20s, I was walking to a bus stop near the University of Auckland in New Zealand. The area was not well lit, so it was very dark and ominous—quite spooky, actually, especially since there was also an old city cemetery across the street. But I was just focused on getting to my bus stop.

Suddenly, out of the blue, a disincarnate voice seemed to come into my head and told me very quickly, sharply, and clearly that a car was about to pull up behind me and a man would try to force me to get inside. I knew to trust this voice.

Literally just seconds after this warning, that's exactly what happened. A rough-looking car pulled up from behind, slowed down, and stopped right in front of me. The man inside verbally and with persuasive hand gestures tried to coerce me into the vehicle. He was unscrupulous and forceful in his manner, and had an awful dark energy about him. He appeared shady, unkempt, and agitated.

It was clear that his intentions were unsavory and that he was not to be trusted. My gut told me to stand back and not get in that car! My angel's warning had calmed me and given me the courage to deal with the situation in a collected manner. I told the man clearly and firmly that I would *not* obey his instructions! Yet he acted as though he wasn't going to waver in his resolve.

But then, in a flash, something suddenly switched in him. Even though the road was completely deserted and there were no people about, he took off in a panic-stricken frenzy. It was as if something had prompted him to go. That would have otherwise been an inconceivable outcome!

I knew that the angels were protecting me from a very serious, dangerous, scary predicament! Their warning helped mentally and emotionally prepare me to deal with such a disturbing occurrence. I dread to think where that man would have taken me, and what he would have done! I might not even be alive today! I often wonder just what the angels did to scare that man away.

While I was shocked—almost in disbelief—once the ordeal was over, I felt lucky, blessed, and protected to have had the angels portend such danger.

∾ ∾ ∾

Chapter 12

SENSING THE PRESENCE OF ANGELS OR DECEASED LOVED ONES

PET REUNION

by Patricia Genetos

My father passed away very recently. Right before Dad died, I asked him to let me know that he was okay. Unexpectedly, though, I became frightened as I lay in bed one night at my brother's house, where Dad had suffered and died in the room downstairs.

The next thing I knew, I felt drowsy, and a pleasant wave of peacefulness came over me, flowing from my toes to my head. I then had a feeling of great joy and heard these six words: "I found Misty. How about that?" It was my father!

Dad had reunited with his beloved little white dog, Misty, in heaven. He knew that I, being quite an animal lover, would relate to what he told me. I smiled and went peacefully to sleep.

A Promise of Love
by Laura M. Mehlhorn

When I was 19 years old, my great-uncle Jim was dying of cancer after years of smoking. The doctors had informed him that he only had a few months left before he would be too ill to travel and would die sedated and in terrible pain.

He wanted to see all of the family one last time before he got too sick. During that last visit, he put his hands on my shoulders, looked me intently in the eyes, and said, "I want you to make me a solemn promise, so don't make it unless you intend to keep it. This is a promise to a dying man, so it's sacred. Promise me that you will never smoke, never even put a cigarette to your lips." He didn't want to have anyone else go through what he was enduring.

Neither of my parents smoked, and I had not yet felt tempted to try it, so I thought it would be an easy promise to keep. I promised him, with loving tears in my eyes, that I wouldn't smoke.

About four years later, I was spending an evening with my fiancé and some of his friends. One of the friends, a smoker himself, suggested that I at least try a cigarette since I never had. I had forgotten my promise. As I took the proffered cigarette between my fingers and considered getting it lit, I felt warm hands on my shoulders and a voice that held such a magnitude of disappointment in it. It said simply: "Oh, but honey, you promised!"

That was all I needed to hear. I instantly knew who was speaking to me, and I remembered the promise. I dropped the cigarette without ever having touched it to my lips, and I've never forgotten the promise again. I am now 53 years old and have a healthy pair of lungs—thanks to my loving great-uncle.

GRANDPA'S LOVING VOICE
by Candice Graham

I was reading psychic medium John Edward's book *One Last Time* and was very intrigued by its content. I was coming back from Florida and was sitting next to my husband on the plane. In the back of the book, there's a meditation you can do to get relaxed enough to have possible contact with someone who has died and gone to the Other Side.

So I tried it, but at the end of the meditation, I thought, *Well, this is not working for me; maybe it's because I'm on a plane with so many people around.* At that very moment, I heard my grandpa's voice, clear as a bell! He said, "I love you, honey!" Tears welled up in my eyes and rushed down my face.

I was so relieved because I knew it was him. And it wasn't scary, like I thought it might have been. It was him—his same voice, with the exact same timbre, and the exact same way he would say it. I have to tell you, it was fantastic. I just said, "I love you, too, Grandpa."

Grandpa was a very religious Christian who went to a strict church where they didn't believe in talking to the dead. So it's ironic that he talked to me from heaven. I believe if you want to contact someone with all your heart and have the love of God in mind, this communication can be as wonderful as it was in the days when the person was here.

One of the reasons why this story is so important to me is that for years I have longed for some validation that heaven really exists. After Grandpa passed, I prayed so hard, "Oh, God, please let there be a heaven that Grandpa is going to." Now I know for certain that heaven truly exists, and that Grandpa is home where he belongs.

❦

AND THE ANGELS SANG
by Susan

In November of 1995, I was living far away from my family. In the middle of the night, I was slowly awakened by beautiful singing. It sounded like a female voice, singing progressively higher-pitched notes. I was now wide-awake, but not at all afraid. Then, the last note was even more high-pitched, with a sense of lightness to it. The music crescendoed and then disappeared into the air.

Since the music sounded like it had come from the living room, I got up and began looking behind all the doors, trying to discover the source of the music. But there was nothing! The next morning, my family called me to say that my grandmother had passed away during the night.

∾ ∾

A NOISE THAT SAVED MY LIFE
by Brenda Gagas

A guardian angel guided me home safely from college one day. The year was 1991, in mid-September. I hadn't gotten much sleep the night before I was to drive home for my sister's wedding. I was tired, exhausted from a night of tossing and turning, with thoughts racing through my head. The drive was over four hours through the Upper Peninsula of Michigan and northern Wisconsin. About two hours into the trip on a two-lane highway, I found myself wanting to take long blinks to rest my eyes. It never occurred to me what would happen if I fell asleep at the wheel.

One long blink ended abruptly with a "thud" on the windshield. I opened my eyes wide, quickly looking to see what I had hit. There was nothing—no marks on the windshield in front of the passenger seat where the noise had come from, no debris flying in the air or rolling on the highway. I knew at that moment that the sound was different from hitting some object. It had too much solid force behind it, just as if someone had pounded a fist on the windshield. I looked in amazement at the passenger seat, knowing in my heart that God had sent an angel to wake me and prevent an accident that could have taken my life and more.

Well, the blood and adrenaline rushing through my body did not keep me awake for long. Within 30 minutes, I felt very tired again. I tried opening the windows and playing the radio loud. But my eyes still wanted to close themselves into a deep sleep while my car hurtled along at 60 miles an hour.

Before I knew it, another "thud" pounded my car. This time, cars were passing by me, and there was a slight curve in the road ahead. With my eyes wide open once again and my heart pounding heavily, I looked in my mirrors to see what had hit me. Nothing. The "thud" came from the left front fender, above my front tire. This time I was wide-awake, praying, and thanking God and my guardian protector.

I knew I was not alone. I couldn't see anything, but I'm still sure to this day that a guardian angel was sitting on the hood of my car, guiding me home safely. In all my life, I have never again heard a "thud" on my car or any car I was a passenger in. Since then, I have never needed to rest my eyes while driving.

∾ ∾

Thank You, Great-Grandma!
by Tracey Staples

When my great-grandmother passed away, I was devastated. She was my best friend, and I always felt a special connection with her. She always knew the right thing to say to make me feel better about everything when no one else could.

I couldn't believe she was gone. I think I really worried my mother because I refused to believe it. I would always have these very "real" dreams about spending time with Great-Grandma. Now I know that I actually *was* spending time with her in my dream state.

But one day I finally realized that she was dead. I was listening to the Barry Manilow song "Can't Smile Without You," and the words just struck me. I wept for days, just as I did right after she passed. The pain and grief were unbearable. On top of my grief, I was deeply panicked and depressed about finding a place to move to. I couldn't bear the thought that she was no longer there to make it better!

A couple of days later, I was at the theater watching a movie. In the middle of the film, I suddenly felt this draft of cold air. When I breathed in, I could smell my great-grandmother. It was a very surreal experience. I was freaked out, but at the same time felt this overwhelming feeling of joy. I looked around the theater to see if there was a source of the draft of cold air, and there wasn't any.

There was no way I could explain the scent, because my great-grandmother always smelled of whatever powder she wore, with Bengay blended in. It was a unique smell! After the incident, I did not encounter it again. I'm someone who always notices details about people—the way they smell, all of their physical features, and how I feel when I'm around them. So my memory of Great-Grandma's smell is very keen, and I'm certain that it was the same one that I sensed in the theater.

All the way home, I was shocked as well as joyful. It was almost like time stood still afterward, and I had this euphoric feeling. I was so pleased that Great-Grandma had let me know she was there.

On Tuesday of that week, my mother called me and said that for some reason she was late for work (which is very unusual for her). Then as she walked out of the apartment building, she ran into the landlord. Now, she hadn't run into her in the whole year she had been living there.

My mother told the landlord that I needed my own place to live, and the woman said that they had one new vacancy. My mother told me, "Now, Tracey, if this isn't a sign you should move into this building, then I don't know what is!" I called the landlord, and I was able to move into the apartment right away. She even allowed me to pay the deposit in installments. Thank you for your help, Great-Grandma!

∾∾

HE KEPT HIS PROMISE
by Peggy L. Lorenz

My husband, Joe, passed away after an eight-month bout with kidney cancer. We had a lot of time to talk about what my future would be like without him, what to do with our children, our business, and many of the little things that we wanted to settle before he passed on.

One of the things that we discussed at great length was our life after the one here on Earth. We were both Christians and believed that our eternity would be spent together with the Lord. But I had a request for my husband. For my own peace of mind, I asked that if there was any way he could let me know that he was okay when he passed over, to please do so, so that I wouldn't worry about him. We were so connected in life that I knew that if he could do this for me, he would. I just had no idea how quickly it would happen.

Joe passed away at 3:35 P.M. on May 14, 1997, surrounded by family and friends. Everyone got to say their final good-byes, and he went very peacefully—he just quit breathing. I had a close friend who stayed with me that night because I really wasn't in any state of mind to be alone, nor did I want to be!

As would be expected, I had a very difficult time falling asleep when everyone finally convinced me that I needed to rest. I was lying on my husband's side of the bed, where Joe breathed his last breath just 12 hours previously. I wasn't asleep, but in that in-between state, where you're still aware of what's going on around you.

I was lying on my side with my hands under my cheek. I felt Joe touch my arm, and I smelled his particular scent. It was a very brief experience, but nonetheless real. I bolted upright in bed and began to cry copiously. It was what I had wanted so badly, but it came so quickly after his death that I was startled and a bit frightened.

At first I thought I was really "losing it." But then I realized that Joe was just fulfilling his promise to me. It's something I will cherish until the day I pass on to be with him.

No Other Explanation
by Lisa Gayle Davis Flores

In 1983, I was hitchhiking from Oregon to Washington to go to my grandpa's funeral. I was standing on the shoulder of the freeway when an El Camino car came onto the shoulder at 55 miles per hour. It struck me in the lower back.

I flew through the air and hit the ground. I really thought I was dead, but then I felt somebody put hands on my shoulders and pick me up. But when I looked to see who had helped me, no one was there. I was also one month pregnant at the time. I believe that this was my guardian angel, saving my unborn child. I will never forget it.

Eternally Blooming
by Barb Hacking

I recently attended a "celebration of life" for Kim, a friend who had passed away after a long illness, leaving behind two young children and a loving husband. One of the speakers at this celebration was her sister, who spoke of how a tulip would now always remind her of Kim. When Kim found out that she probably wouldn't be alive in the spring, she planted lots of tulip bulbs. What a cheerful reminder each spring of her love for her family!

When I returned home that night, I went into my seven-year-old daughter's bedroom to read her a story. Before I started, Rachel leaned over and told me I smelled like tulips. Wow! Children really are so in tune to what is going on around them. She had not been to the celebration, and she had no idea about the legacy of tulips that Kim had left behind.

An Angel's Kiss
by Maya Tonisson

My romantic partner passed away on June 18, 1999, at the age of 26. He had suffered a hemorrhage in his brain, and after an operation and one week in a coma in intensive care, he let himself go. I was 25, and beside myself, having never experienced losing a partner—or for that matter, anyone in my life who was so young. He was pronounced dead at about 5 or 6 A.M., and I stayed with a friend that night, not wanting to be alone.

The following evening, however, I chose to stay home by myself, and after I got into bed, I reached a state of "twilight sleep." I was half-awake, half-asleep, when I felt my partner lie beside me, and he kissed me very softly. After a few moments, I jolted awake, sitting up and opening my eyes, and he was gone. I never saw him, but I still believe to this day that what I felt was real.

Chapter 13

ANGEL LIGHTS

THE CHOICE
by Christine Sinon

When I was pregnant with my first child, I lived on a small island in Micronesia—Pohnpei.

I'd gotten up to use the outhouse in the middle of the night. Nobody else in the house was awake. I left the door ajar because it always got stuck, and I didn't want to wake everybody up when I came back. As I returned to the house, I felt a silence around me, as if I were separated from the house.

The front door had been closed and locked—at least *I* couldn't open it—but nobody was awake inside. I tapped lightly, thinking that whoever closed the door would still be awake and let me in, but nobody stirred and nobody heard me. It was as if we were separated by some invisible barrier. I walked around to the back door, looked in our bedroom window, and tried to wake my husband.

Once in the backyard, I felt a multitude of spiritual presences around and above me, not threatening in any way, but perhaps curious. I saw many points of light that looked like stars, but they were very close to me in the night air, probably about six feet off the ground (I am 5'3"), and I felt as if the spirits were just slightly above my head. Although I didn't see anything concrete, I somehow knew that they were spirits of dead relatives of my husband.

I felt that they were asking if I wanted one of them to be reincarnated as the soul of the baby I was carrying. At the time, I did not believe in reincarnation. I tried to shrug these feelings off and attempted to get back in the house. I knocked louder and even called out, but the people in the house didn't hear me. I felt that if I didn't make some kind of choice, I would be stuck outside all night. I was starting to feel scared.

Finally, I said aloud, "I don't want any of you. I don't even know any of you. You're being too pushy. I'll take someone who's sitting up there in a corner somewhere who gave up on ever having another chance at life on Earth a long time ago!"

And in that instant, the night sounds returned. I walked to the front door, and it was ajar, just as I had left it. And the next morning, nobody admitted to having gotten up, closed, locked, and then opened the door.

∾∾

LIGHTS OF PURITY AND JOY
by Jonathan Robinson

Several years ago, some friends and I went to the Anza-Borrego Desert, about 100 miles east of San Diego. Our plan was to spend several days hiking and meditating. After a day of hiking, we found a very remote spot and started to set up camp for the night.

My spiritual teacher had told me that angelic beings sometimes visited this area, and that they could sometimes be attracted by the playing of music. He had given my friend and me wooden flutes, even though neither of us knew how to play them. He told us to find a place that felt comfortable and learn how to play a simple song together.

We became very engrossed in trying to play our flutes. After about an hour, the air seemed to start vibrating around us. My friend and I looked up and saw five balls of light surrounding us. The lights were different colors and sizes, ranging from a couple feet to perhaps seven feet in diameter. At first I thought I was hallucinating, but then I saw my friend pointing to the same balls of light I was seeing. We were in awe.

The balls of light started to make childlike noises, as if they were playing with us by bouncing around our heads. They seemed to emanate a vibration of purity, innocence, and just plain fun.

∾ ∾

WHITE LIGHTS AND THE MIRACULOUS RECOVERY
by Donna DeRuvo

My seven-year-old son, Joseph, was very ill. I was naturally very concerned about his recovery, and worried that he would have long-term damage from his illness if his medication did not work. I prayed every day, asking God to send as many angels as possible to heal and protect him. I prayed that the Archangel Raphael would surround Joseph in his green light of healing. I prayed morning, noon, and night, trying not to doubt, especially when I looked at Joseph's limp body sleeping in my bed.

One afternoon, Joey asked me to lie down with him, complaining of feeling worse than ever. He cried in pain, and I cried in fear. Again, I began to pray, stronger than ever before. As I closed my eyes, I began to see little white lights in the darkness. I assumed that there was something in my eyes, or that I was seeing things. I opened my eyes to focus and kept seeing these lights. I can't really describe this, but it was beautiful all around the room. I kept looking, not understanding what I was seeing. But as suddenly as they appeared, they disappeared.

The next day, Joey woke up feeling much better. He had a quick recovery, with no lasting symptoms. I thank the angels and God.

~~~

ILLUMINATION
by Lisa Crofts

On December 8, 1994, at 7:50 P.M., I was on my way to visit a friend whom I had not seen in years. I was 23 years old. Just a week before, I had bought a beautiful bumper sticker that I hadn't yet put on my car. It read: "CAUTION: NEVER DRIVE FASTER THAN YOUR ANGELS CAN FLY!" Those words stood out in my mind so much that I was only going 5 miles over the 50-mile-per-hour speed limit.

Just as I approached the crest of a hill, a dark vehicle passed me going the opposite way. When I looked back in front of me, I saw a huge cloud of dirt. I then saw something I will never forget in my entire life: a car was coming straight at me! I thought, *Oh my God, I'm going to die!*

At the moment just before impact, the other car became illuminated in a glorious white light, and I had a moment of clarity. I knew I would not die, but that the person in the other car *would,* and that I was going to be in a great deal of pain. The other car exploded on impact. I was hit hard, and fortunately I was wearing my seat belt and had an air bag.

With flaming debris flying everywhere, I crawled out of my car's passenger side. I saw people trapped in the other car. I had to help them! I took only a few steps when my legs gave out. I found out later that I had a broken ankle.

I watched helplessly as other passersby tried in vain to save the young driver's life, but he burned to death there on the side of the road. He was only 24. It was learned later that he had been passing many cars, and when he tried to pass the last one, a race started because the dark vehicle got that "You can't pass me" attitude. That's where I came in, and my life changed forever.

It took me a while to understand the vision of the white light until I talked with the woman who had sold me the bumper sticker. She said that the white light was my angel helping me get through the trauma. What an amazing thought for me to contemplate. Not that I don't believe in angels, but nothing like that had ever happened to me! I know now that my vision helped me more than I can ever understand, and I will be forever grateful for my angels' help.

ESCORTED BY ANGELS
by Elaine M. Elkins

My husband and I were flying to Reno, Nevada, for some fun. I am so terrified to fly that I always take a pill to calm me in the air. On the Reno flight, though, I had forgotten to bring a pill with me. The flight was becoming progressively bumpier. I could feel the plane dropping altitude and then climbing. The pilot apologized for the turbulence and said he was trying different altitudes, yet nothing was working. The flight crew was ordered to sit down and buckle up.

I told my husband that I was terrified, and I didn't think we were going to make it. He was the picture of calmness. I thought for sure that the plane was going to go down. I had never experienced anything like it, and I was so mad for forgetting to take my pill. He gave me a book to read to take my mind off the flight, but I wondered how anyone could read at such a time. He said, "You really need to read this book; it will help," and he handed me a copy of *Angel Therapy*.

I read that Raphael will come with you when you travel and help you arrive at your destination safely. So I silently told the archangel,

I am terrified, scared silly. Please be here to help this plane land safely. Still, I didn't feel anything but fear. Then I read that you can call a thousand angels, and they will be there. So I silently prayed, *I am really scared; I want to return home to my children. My daughter needs me. I need a thousand angels here. I need to know you are here.*

I was staring out the window, and all of a sudden I saw little bright dots on it. At first, I thought it was that light you see in your peripheral vision. So I stared. As I continued to look, I could see definite patterns of light coming up into a starburst and trailing down like fireworks, only to fall to the bottom of the window and then form another starburst.

I also saw the little dancing lights form a circle and spin. For the longest time, I watched these patterns on the windows. My husband asked what I was doing. I smiled and replied, "I'm watching the angels." I then felt that we were going to be okay. I watched the angels play for the rest of the flight and realized that the plane was going to make it. It did, thanks to Raphael and his band of angels.

We had a wonderful time in Reno with our friends. On the flight home, I kept staring at the window. It was a wonderful flight—no turbulence at all. I realized that the reason I didn't see the lights was because I felt safe and knew we would be home soon. The angels were there, and they were wonderful.

Steam-Room Angels
by Stephanie Gunning

I had recently learned a new way to pray, and because I am an endless experimenter, I wanted to test how effective it was. It's not that I am a spiritual skeptic; it's just that I got excited. I had been told there are four important steps to prayer:

1. Find a sanctuary.
2. Breathe into the prayer.
3. Admit your vulnerability.
4. Ask for what you want or need as if your prayer has already been answered.

The next afternoon, I worked out at the gym and decided to take a steam bath. Lying on my back on a towel, alone and naked in the steam room, I remembered the list of prayer steps I'd just been taught. *Well, I couldn't find more of a sanctuary,* I thought. And for sure, I was in a vulnerable position. Plus, if I prayed in the dark, no one who entered the steam room would realize what I was doing; and while I was alone, I could talk out loud to make extra sure I was "doing it right."

I decided to pray for my soul mate to find me. I had indulged in the fantasy of finding a partnership similar to the one that two friends of mine had, but my idealism was shattered when my friends divorced and the husband committed suicide. Since then, it seemed as if soul mates weren't real.

First, I breathed deeply into my body and admitted my vulnerability. "Dear God and Divine Mother," I prayed, "here I am. I am a woman alone in the world. There are so many reasons why." Then I listed my reasons. I added, "I am so very lonely sometimes." I explained that I had lost my ideal of marriage, and I prayed for peace over the loss of my friend who took his own life. I continued praying in minute detail, leaving nothing out.

All at once in the darkness, I almost felt a change of atmosphere. I was so intent on prayer and breath and being openhearted that I had entered into an intense, highly focused state of being. Through the clouds of steam, with my eyes closed, I saw a pulsing, dark red spiral of energy envelop me. It was not frightening, but comforting. I burst into tears. Then there were shoots of bright green piercing the field of energy throbbing around me, and swirling mists of rich purple.

I intuitively knew that each light was a separate being, and it was so humbling that they had come to be with me in my time of need and vulnerability. I felt tremendously connected to the Divine, and I knew without a doubt that the light was a friend who had come to reassure me. I felt entirely loved by heaven's angels.

Once connected, I continued my prayer, which became a statement of gratitude for my soul mate who I know will find me. I believe it. Since that day, I haven't felt lonely, or anxious about the future and finding love. I look people in the eye to see their souls and establish a clear connection. When my soul mate arrives, on or behind schedule—or even if I miss him here on Earth this time around—that's okay. As my steam-room angels helped me understand, love is everywhere.

<hr />

SAVED BY THE LIGHT
by Mili Ponesse

I was driving home from work one day. I was 16 years old and had just received my driver's license. I stopped at a red light. In a hurry, I impatiently waited for the light to turn green so that I could take off quickly.

All of a sudden, though, my focus shifted from that traffic light. From out of nowhere, a bright light similar to sun glare brought my attention to the side of the road. I just sat there, transfixed by the light, almost daydreaming, but not thinking of anything. I was startled when the driver behind me honked his horn. The traffic light had turned green, and I hadn't noticed.

However, before I could collect myself, a truck flew through the red light, crossing my path at about 70 miles an hour. If I'd gone through that light as soon as it turned green, I would have been hit by that speeding truck and been in an extremely bad accident.

I know that an angel saw the danger coming my way and distracted me with the bright light to keep me from driving through the intersection. I know it was an angel because of the comfort and warmth I felt the rest of my "slow" ride home.

~~~

Guardian on the Road
by Douglas Lockhart

My wife and I were truck drivers. One night we were crossing the border between Arizona and New Mexico. My wife was lying down in the sleeper, and I was driving. It was about 3 A.M., and I was very tired, but there was no time to stop and sleep because our job required us to get the freight from point A to point B.

I continued to drive, and I don't know if I fell asleep at the wheel, but the next thing I knew, a great white ball of light came from the blackened night sky and passed through me. It blew my hair back, and I immediately felt as refreshed as if I had slept for ten hours. It was the most amazing thing that has ever happened to me.

~~~

The Light of My Mother's Love and Wisdom
by Judith Mitchell

I was 41 when my mother unexpectedly passed away. I was overwhelmed with grief and loss. Her passing made me realize that I was unsure of my own spiritual beliefs and that I did not like my feeling of aloneness. One night while I was trying to sleep, my mother came to me as a spinning ball of red light. I knew that it was her!

I could actually put my hand into this light. I was filled with such a sense of love. She let me know that I was never alone, and that she loved me and was always with me. Mom also told me that love and the circle of life were very important, that there are many spirits around me all the time, and that life goes on. Mostly, she helped me understand that she was fine and happy.

My mother was raised a Catholic, so many people had asked, "Was she saved?" Well, Mom let me know that we are *all* saved. That was not an issue. She helped me see that there are so many paths that lead to the same place. I had always fought my gift of seeing and knowing, and now I am so thankful to be assured that I am not alone, that life goes on, and that change is good. My mother's visit transformed my life for the better and put me on a greater spiritual path. I know I may call on her anytime and that she is with me.

I no longer feel the pain of missing her, for I know she is with me always. My whole outlook on life has improved now, and I am open to receiving the help that is there for me if I need it. The love is always there. I am so grateful for this wonderful glimpse of the afterlife that I've been given. I thank God for it.

"THANK YOU, RAPHAEL!"
by Sue Barrie

I am a 47-year-old mother of three boys, and I've just made it through the worst three years of my life! I truly believe that I've been guided, carried, comforted, and healed by the angels that surround me.

Three years ago, my husband and I divorced; then I moved, and my two oldest sons left home. Throughout these stressful times, I relied more and more on spiritual help. I had always believed that we all have guardian angels. On two occasions when I felt I couldn't take any more, I felt a hand ever so gently stroke my cheek, and once I felt someone patting me on the head very softly.

A few months later, I discovered a lump in my breast. I instinctively knew that it was cancer, but for some reason I felt calm and had the knowledge that I would beat it. I asked my angels each night for healing and strength, and each day, I woke up with an inner confidence.

My mastectomy went well, and I came home two days after surgery. I barely took a painkiller as I prayed regularly to Archangel Raphael, and I was visited and comforted on two occasions.

The first night, I woke up with a little discomfort, feeling a bit lonely and sorry for myself. But then as I stirred, I felt the sensation of arms wrapped around the upper parts of my legs, as though someone was holding me close to comfort me. I went back to sleep instantly.

The following night, I was having difficulty finding a comfortable position in which to sleep. I had just completed my prayer for healing when I detected the distinct smell of coconut oil! Then I heard a sort of shuffle in my room in a corner to the right of me.

I turned onto my back, and as I did so, I got a tremendous shock. High above me on my ceiling were dozens of tiny twinkling lights, almost like miniature glowworms. They wiggled and shone only in the area directly above me! I was awestruck and elated, as I knew at that moment that I had been visited by my angels, and the healing was beginning both spiritually and physically for me!

I feel so full of love and joy these days, and I see beauty in everything. This has made me so excited that I tell everyone I can about this tremendous power and love! My biopsies show that there is no more cancer, and I'm overjoyed.

Chapter 14

SIGNS FROM ABOVE

THE LITTLE CROSS
by Tuihana Marsh

A couple of months ago, I went to pick my daughter up from her friend's house after school, which was our normal routine. When I pulled into the driveway, she ran out of the house and jumped into the truck. I asked her about her friend's new dog and if she could bring it out so I could see it. She told me that the dog wasn't allowed outside because it was wet and I should go in and have a look.

I hesitated . . . I had a weird feeling, but I couldn't place it. I ended up jumping out to go knock on the front door. While my back was turned, the pickup rolled down the driveway, which was on a hill. On its way out onto the road, it hit another car; then, as I ran after it, it went straight across the road up onto the opposite sidewalk and hit a street sign, cutting it clean in half. Finally it stopped, after rolling back onto the road in front of traffic. (The circumstances could not have been worse, as it was rush hour, on a main road, and it was raining.)

The most dangerous part of the whole thing was that the passenger side of the vehicle, where my daughter was sitting, was facing the oncoming traffic. The whole time this was happening my poor girl was sitting paralyzed, unsure of what to do, as she rolled away from me!

All the cars swerved in the rain or skidded to a stop . . . no one was hurt! After all the drama with the owner of the hit vehicle subsided, we finally left the scene. As we got back into the truck, we both noticed a little cross sitting by the gearshift. Everything else that was in the pickup had been thrown clear to the back of the vehicle or under the seats . . . but this little cross sat perfectly in place, as if it had been deliberately set there.

The night before, I had been flipping through one of Doreen's books (I think it was *My Guardian Angel*) and skimmed over a couple of stories about vehicle angels and how you should ask for protection before getting into a car. In the morning, I kept flashing back to the things I had read, and I had intended to stop and ask the angels to watch over my girl while she was at school, but kept getting sidetracked and never did it.

When the accident happened, I was so furious with myself. I should have known to pay attention to the stories from the night before, my urge to ask for protection in the morning, and the odd feeling I had before jumping out of the truck . . . but I'd brushed it all off.

I never said anything about this to my daughter. I was too busy reproaching myself for how careless I had been—how I should have spoken to her at some point about how to pull on the hand brake, stomp on the brake pedal, or turn the steering wheel! All I could think was: *If I had only taken the time to stop and ask that my daughter be protected, this would not have happened.*

In the middle of my thoughts, my daughter piped up: "I know the only reason I'm okay is because the angels were looking after me!"

She was right. I had been too busy blaming myself to see that all was well and yes, the angels *had* looked after my baby anyway! We both feel that the little cross was telling us this very clearly.

That's my experience of the angels saving my daughter—who is the love of my life—and teaching me a thing or two in the process!

❧❧

An Angel Who Descended from the Clouds
by Susan Moore

My grandmother was in the hospital for major heart surgery, with a 50-50 chance of survival. After surgery, she never woke up from the anesthesia, and she was in a coma for two weeks. I lived about 90 minutes away from the hospital, and I visited her every other day with my mother. One particular day, though, I didn't want to make the long drive to the hospital, so I stayed home. I was horrified when Grandma passed away at 5 A.M. the next day. This really bothered me, because I didn't get to see her one final time.

That evening, I went into the kitchen in the dark, looking out the back door. I said aloud, "Why did you leave me? I didn't get to say good-bye or even give you one last kiss!" I started to cry again . . . then something caught my attention.

I saw this funnel-shaped cloud come down from the sky. It almost looked like a tornado was heading my way. Then this funnel cloud started to take shape, and I stood mesmerized as it turned into a beautiful woman! She had long white hair and a long white dress on, with some sort of rope tied around her waist.

Then she started to reach out with her arms and float toward me. She was suspended about five feet off the ground, and she was about six feet tall. When she lifted her arms, her long sleeves were hanging and flapping in the wind. Once she got about three feet in front of me, I took off! I was petrified, so I ran to get my husband to come see this. I knew that no one would believe me, so I wanted him to witness this amazing sight.

When I finally got him, though, she was gone, and the only thing left was a thick fog sitting about two feet above the ground.

Then we looked at our neighbors' homes, and we were the only house with fog in the backyard. I truly believe that this was an angel coming to let me know that my grandmother was okay and in a better place. I often wonder what would have happened if I had stayed to see the angel instead of running. It has been five years since this happened, and I can still see the vision in my mind as if it happened yesterday.

The Purple-Haired Angel
by Leanne Hernandez

My grandmother died in 1998, shortly before my daughter's fifth birthday. In her younger days, my grandmother was known for being quite eccentric—she had even dyed her hair lavender for many years.

I was out of town on a business trip, so my mother helped me get ready for my daughter's birthday party by ordering a cake with a brunette angel on it. When she went to pick it up, she was amazed to find that the baker had used lavender icing for the angel's hair. My mother asked, "Who ever heard of an angel with purple hair?" I knew that this was my grandmother's way of telling us that she had made it to heaven and was with us in spirit to celebrate my daughter's special day.

SAFE AND SOUND
by Suzanne Chaney

My husband and I were driving in a small rental car from Kentucky to New York City. The first part of the trip was very nice and quite scenic. But as we started nearing the peaks of the Appalachians, the skies grew increasingly more ominous. Soon we were driving in heavy snow, on slick roads. We slowed our pace to a crawl, but large semitrucks kept blowing past us, and the wind they created pushed us all over the road. The sides of the roads were marked with No Stopping signs, so we continued as best we could. We were incredibly scared.

At that time, I said a prayer for God to send angels to help us on our journey, to bless those driving with good judgment, and to protect us from danger. Immediately after raising my head from the prayer, I looked out my window at the storm clouds.

In the midst of the dark, looming sky was one bright white cloud in the shape of an angel's face. It also had glowing, luminescent wings. The sun peeked above the edges of this cloud so that it shone brightly, with beams of bright light shooting from its edges. My eyes swelled with tears, and I knew that my prayer had been answered.

We spent two more hours traveling on the snow-slicked roads, but it was an entirely different experience. The semis' wind no longer seemed to affect our car. Throughout the two-hour period, I continued to glimpse angels in the clouds, but nothing as brilliant as the first sighting.

The clouds seemed to be a sign from the angels, saying, "We're still here with you." The fear left my heart. We arrived safely in New York City several hours later, and despite the grueling drive, I felt invigorated and light, like everything in the world was right. Such a glorious gift we received!

THE COMFORTING ANGEL CLOUD
by Rebecca Powers

My father was dying of cancer. It was near the end, and we had him at home, comfortable and in no pain. He was comatose, but I knew that he was aware we were with him. I was having a hard time dealing with the whole "death" thing, and I was afraid for him—afraid of what he was feeling, and of what he was about to go through. I wanted to make sure he would be okay and not be alone, but I needed some sort of answer, some sort of sign. I had none, and I was afraid.

It was a typical October night, and my family and I were waiting—*praying*—for the end. I went out on the front step to get some fresh air. I sat down and said a little prayer. I pleaded, "Please, please, give me some sort of sign, any sign, just so I'll know he'll be okay."

At that very moment, I looked into the sky at the beautiful sunset, and I saw an angel—plain as day, clear to my human eyes. It was a beautiful cloud—a beautiful angel. There was my answer.

I ran inside, got my mother, and grabbed a camera. We both sat there and wept. I took a picture of the angel; then she disappeared. My father passed away ten minutes later. The angel had come to take him home. At that point I knew, I really *knew* . . . that he was okay. My father was not alone, and he was with that beautiful angel, going home. I have the picture of the angel and will send it to anyone who doesn't believe. I believe. I will *always* believe.

HAPPY IN HEAVEN
by Helen

My 24-year-old son died on August 14, 1999. His presence is sorely missed, as he had lived at home with us while he was attending college. Thoughts of my son consume my mind almost every moment of every given day, even though I am wholly functioning.

One evening shortly after Thanksgiving, I was having a very difficult moment while alone in my home. I was drawn to the window, since the container holding my son's ashes was sitting on the window seat. (We were going to be spreading his ashes over the ocean soon.) As I put my fingertips on the container, missing him and talking to him while softly crying, I noticed that the moon was very low in the sky and extremely bright.

I suddenly became aware that a cloud had appeared; and in the short time I was standing by the window, the outline of a complete angel formed, with large rounded wings on each side of a delicate body wearing a flowing gown, and footlike clouds that hung below the gown! It was a most comforting sight for me, and I felt momentarily at peace. I had a sense that my son, who probably feels for me, was trying to relay that he is with the angels and that they are taking good care of him in heaven.

❦❦

A Sign from Uncle Frank
by Angie Chiste

Frank, my uncle, died in 1984, and my son was born in 1991. My son has had a longtime fascination with his deceased great-uncle. When he was about four years old, he would tell me how Uncle Frank would come to him at the playground at his day-care center and push him on the swing or talk to him.

I decided to give my son a little test. He had never seen a photo of Uncle Frank. I showed him pictures of all my other uncles first; then I showed him one of Uncle Frank . . . and my son knew exactly who he was! I thought he must have a special bond of some sort with him.

When my son entered first grade in 1996, we would drive past the cemetery on our way to and from school each day. He would ask me questions about Uncle Frank, and then one day he told me that he wanted to visit his grave. I asked my mother where he was buried, and she could only give me the name of that corner in the cemetery.

One day I picked my son up from school and we headed to the cemetery. We walked up and down among the headstones, looking for my uncle. It was a cool fall day and very still. After about 45 minutes of searching, my son started to whine; he was getting hungry. I was losing my patience. We were both growing tired and cranky. I finally looked up to the sky and said, "Sorry, Uncle Frank, I just can't find you today. We'll come back another day."

Just then, a huge gust of wind stirred the leaves behind me, which caused me to turn around. The moment I turned, the wind stopped. I looked down and there was my uncle's grave. Right at my feet!

THE MESSAGE FROM THE ROSE PETALS
by Bonnie Suzanne Koester

I was having some difficulty at a small college where I worked. There was a lot of politics among the employees, including my boss, and things got so bad that I considered quitting my job. I prayed for guidance.

As was my routine, one morning I went to the convenience store next to the college for breakfast. On this particular day, I found some red rose petals lying on the grass between the campus and the store. I picked one up and smiled, inwardly asking, *Is this from my angels?* But then I concluded that someone must have thrown the petals there. I took one back to my office and placed it on the base of my lamp.

The next morning I came in, and the petal had shriveled. I went to the store, and there on the grass in the same place were fresh pink rose petals. There was no sign of the red ones. I furrowed my brow and thought, *How could I have missed these yesterday, and who is doing this?* And why would someone be throwing rose petals on the ground? I was trying my best to think of a logical explanation.

I picked up one of the pink petals, and as I walked across the parking lot, returning to my office, I smelled the scent of roses so strongly that it made my eyes widen. I thought, *A single petal would not give off this scent.* I raised my hand to my nose and smelled the petal. I smelled nothing but the scent of my hand. I took it away, and again there was that strong smell of roses!

Pasadena, Texas, where I live and work, has oil refineries. The air here *never* smells like roses. I knew beyond a shadow of a doubt that these were signs from my angels.

I took this petal and placed it alongside the withered red one. The next day, the pink had withered as well. I returned once again to the spot . . . and there I found both red and pink petals, and they were fresh. With a smile, I said, "Okay, okay, I'll tough it out. I'll stay here a bit longer. Thank you. You guys are too much!"

The angels were right—I now have a new position at the college and have almost doubled my income. And I still have the petals.

A Sign of Protection
by Micci DeBonis

My mother, Katherine, had just purchased a new car, so for good luck, I gave her an angel clip that went on the sun visor.

On this particular day, my mother was watching my six-month-old daughter while I was at work. While on an outing in Mom's new car, they stopped for gasoline.

They were waiting in line at the gas pumps, and my daughter was making a fuss in the backseat. My mother turned around to see what the problem was and noticed that my daughter needed her bottle, so she turned to get it. Right then, she saw a car coming straight toward her! The man hit the front of Mom's car, completely totaling it. The air bag deployed, and luckily she wasn't hurt and neither was my baby.

After the police reports were completed, Mom went back to the car and noticed that the angel clip was missing from the visor. Looking all over the car, she finally found the clip: it had landed in the backseat where my daughter was in her car seat. I truly believe that angels played a part in assuring the safety of my mother and daughter. The police officer said that if my mother had been a couple of feet closer to the gas tanks, the outcome would not have been very good.

There were angels around my mother and daughter during that ordeal, and Mom and I thank them every day.

A Call from My Angel
by Suzanne Goodnough

My husband and I attended Doreen's seminar at the Whole Life Expo in Chicago in October of 1999. At one point during the seminar, Doreen took everyone in the audience through a meditation, where we asked the guardian angel on our left to say his/her name to us. Then we proceeded with the guardian angel on the right. She instructed us not to judge what we heard and not to let our egos get in the way.

Doreen told us that if we didn't believe what we heard, then we should ask for a sign of validation from the particular angel and wait to see what happens. After the seminar, I asked my husband if he had gotten any names. He said, "Yes, the names Michael and Philip. Did you hear any?"

"Yes," I replied. "The angel on the right said her name was Grace." I loved it—the name was so spiritual and angelic that I never questioned it. But the angel on the left had said his name was Maurice. In my mind, I said, *Maurice! What a stupid name for an angel!* It made me think of Maurice Gibb of the Bee Gees, and I imagined a *Saturday Night Fever* disco angel, with a strobe light, white suit, and the works. I thought, *This can't be! I don't want a disco angel!*

That night during my evening prayers and meditation, I asked the angels for a sign. I said, *Please give me a sign that I just didn't make up the name Maurice.* The next morning at 8 o'clock, the telephone rang. We were still sleepy, so I didn't answer, and the answering machine picked up the message.

When I retrieved the message, a male voice said, "I am looking to speak with Suzanne Goodnough. My name is Maurice. If you call this number and ask for this extension, I will be able to help you with your problem and get it all cleared up in two minutes. Looking forward to hearing from you." I saved the message so that my husband could listen to it.

I said to my husband, "Out of all the male names, can you believe this man's is Maurice?" I returned the call shortly after and asked for the extension the man had given in the message. A woman answered the phone. I told her who I was and asked to speak to Maurice.

She said, "My dear, I don't know who you talked to, but there is no one by the name of Maurice who works here." After that, I believed that my angel's name is Maurice.

(**Author's note:** I was editing this story while on a Eurostar train, and twice, after this story was complete, I looked up to see the name Maurice on a building sign!)

A Sign from the Blessed Mother
by Antoinette Voll

My mom, age 66, was having a hard time breathing whenever she climbed stairs or walked up hills. It got to the point where it was getting more and more difficult. Since I had lost my dad just 18 months earlier, we were all walking on eggshells. Medical tests were finally conducted, showing that she had two coronary blockages. Our family doctor referred my mom to a hospital where they could perform an exploratory procedure to see the extent of the blockage.

One week before my mom's appointment, I started praying earnestly to the Blessed Mother. I would talk to her picture and pray that she either make the blockages disappear or please give me strength to handle this next crisis. So when my mother went to the hospital that morning, her sister stayed with me, and we prayed.

When the procedure was over, the doctor at the hospital asked why my mother was having this test. The exploratory procedure showed that her arteries were in perfect condition, with no blockage whatsoever. I told him to ask our family doctor. When our family doctor came down, they all had the strangest looks. There was no logical answer.

As the attendants were wheeling my mother down to the hospital ward, they found out that all the beds were taken and they had to put her at the nurses' station. As they parked her near the window of the station, right above her head was the same picture of the Blessed Mother that I had prayed to all week. Did my spirits ever soar! It was the most amazing feeling. We truly witnessed a miracle, and the Blessed Mother showed me her picture to reassure me that she had intervened!

DANIEL
by Charmaine Jabr

My 44-year-old brother, Daniel, passed away from liver illness. He had abused drugs and alcohol all of his adult life, and as a result, made some terrible mistakes that affected many people. I loved him just the same, and always wondered what happened to his soul when he died.

It was around the time of his birthday, and Elton John's song "Daniel" was on the car radio. Hearing my brother's name in the song's lyrics brought me to tears. I begged God to give me a sign to let me know what happened to Dan's soul. Well, just then, a pickup truck pulled up in front of me and had the most awesome mural painted on it. On the left side of the tailgate was a dark, stormy, dreary-looking scene; and on the right side was Jesus floating up in the clouds into heaven. Then I read the license plate frame; it said: JESUS WON.

From that day on, the immense grief I felt over the loss of my brother was lifted. His childhood was filled with so much pain that the odds were against him from the start. He suffered terribly in this life, yet he had such spirit and charm that he could only be somewhere better. Now I know that for sure.

HEALING ANGEL
by Lily Alexandrovitch

On February 21, 1996, my cousin Cindy; her husband, Michael; my brother; and I went to the Ethel M chocolate factory in Las Vegas, Nevada. It had been raining all day and was still drizzling when we went into the factory. After purchasing chocolates, the three of them wanted to tour the grounds, while I went to sit in the car, since it was chilly outside. All the other cars and tour buses had left. Although the sky above was still thick with dark clouds, it had stopped raining. Sitting in the backseat, I looked out the side window on my right and noticed a beautiful, majestic mountain range that extended from behind the building on the left to behind the chocolate factory on the right.

The mountains were dark gray and purplish. The sky above them was light blue, although above the car it was still hidden behind dark clouds. It looked as though the sun had just set behind the mountains, and the entire ridge had a white glow above it. I couldn't help thinking how unusual it was, and that I had never seen anything like it. If anyone had painted an exact picture of the scene, everyone would say it was all wrong. I must have stared at this beautiful mountain for at least 20 minutes. Then my friends returned to the car.

I never said anything; I just continued looking at the mountains, since I was so mesmerized by them. No one spoke a word; we all just sat there and stared at them. Then Michael said, "If anyone painted a picture of the mountains looking like that, they would be told they had it all wrong, as it's too bright to be real"—my exact thoughts! We were all quiet and just kept looking. Around the middle of our view, the mountain range dipped down and then upward, forming a large V. The sky behind the V was now also pale blue. Although I had never taken my eyes away, I now saw two glowing rays that looked like gigantic spotlights coming from behind the V in the mountain, up toward the sky.

Then right in the middle of these two rays, a white speck appeared. The speck quickly got bigger, and it now looked like a cloud, except that it was exceptionally bright. The cloud then started to take shape, first resembling a person, and then with wings on either side of it. It was an angel—a huge angel with large wings! The angel was turned slightly to the right. I suddenly thought that maybe I was the only one witnessing this incredible sight, and without taking my eyes off it, I said, "I see an angel."

"It sure looks like an angel," said Michael. We sat in awe, just staring.

Remembering that Cindy had never had any religious training, I asked what she saw. Nervously laughing, she said, "I see an angel."

A few seconds later, the angel quickly shrank into a dot and then vanished into the pale blue sky where it had originated. What a memorable experience!

∾ ∾

A Tiny Miracle
by Cammi Collier

My husband and I went to Sedona, Arizona, Christmas week. We were taking a walk one night, and the moon was brilliant and comforting. However, I was cold, and my nose was running! I said to my husband, "I know this angel stuff works when I'm alone. Let's see if it works with *you* here, too!"

I said a prayer for a tissue to blow my nose. I've learned that no request is too trivial for the angels. Right away, I heard the angels tell me to look toward the right side of the road. Sure enough, about three feet ahead of us on the right were two clean facial tissues. Although I believe in miracles, I am still thrilled when I witness them. The tissues were new, thick, and soft, with a lotion scent.

I thanked the angels for their love and generosity. It's comforting to know that they can even take care of runny noses!

∾ ∾

An Abundant Sign
by Elles Taddeo

Several years ago, my husband had some frightening physical symptoms, and we were very concerned that his condition might be serious. He was scheduled to go to the doctor and have some medical tests performed. One afternoon when I was at the park with my son, I felt especially worried about my husband's health. I asked my guardian angel to let me know if everything would be okay.

I said to the angels, "Please let me find a four-leaf clover as a sign that things are fine with my husband." I sat down in the grass with my son, looked down, and there was my four-leaf clover! I picked it and happily showed it to my son. Then I looked down again at the same spot and saw another four-leaf clover. Delighted, I picked it up and remarked how unusual this was. I pointed to the spot where it came from to show my son, and we saw *another* one! And another, and another! I picked a total of 27 four-leaf clovers from the same little patch of grass! The next day, I found five more in my own backyard! I dried them all and still have them.

The angels must have thought something like, *Okay, you want a four-leaf clover, you'll get four-leaf clovers!* Although I later tried to find my magic patch again, I never could. Needless to say, all my husband's tests went fine, and there was nothing wrong with him.

All You Have to Do Is Ask
by Reta

It had been a really busy day. I had an interview for a position that I truly felt was mine, but there were some obstacles that would have to be overcome along the way. I took a vacation day, had a midmorning massage, came home, and prepared for the series of interviews to follow.

That evening, I had considerable trouble calming down. I knew that the next day would be truly grueling, complete with a nearly four-hour drive, two morning meetings, followed by another almost four hours on the road for a late-afternoon meeting, and another 90-minute drive back home. About the time I was giving up on falling asleep, I decided to visit Doreen's website.

I'll never forget this visit to **www.AngelTherapy.com**. I read an article Doreen wrote called "You Are Surrounded by Angels." I needed that reinforcement. I reread it and felt my composure return. As I walked away from my computer and went into my living room on my way to bed, I thought, *In some way, I have experienced every one of the angel manifestations Doreen spoke of, but I don't remember finding any unexplained feathers. That would be a really awesome experience!*

The next morning came quickly. On my way out of town, I went to my office to write a thank-you note to the interviewers and pick up the files I would need that day. As I left, I was so confident that I locked the door without a second glance. A stop at the restroom was appropriate due to the length of the drive ahead. As I turned on the bathroom light, I noticed that there was something on my skirt. I was quite annoyed, because returning home and changing was going to cost about an hour. I tried to brush off whatever it was . . . and stopped in my tracks—I realized that I was looking at feathers on my skirt!

Of course, this made me feel cared for and loved and supported. I had gotten my angel feathers, and all I had to do was ask.

∾∾∾

PART II

How You Can

Encounter

Angels

Chapter 15

BEING RECEPTIVE
TO HEAVEN

We all have angel encounters continually, but many of us aren't aware of these occurrences. They can be subtle, that's for sure. So in this section, we'll explore how to bring your heavenly connections to the level of conscious awareness. When you're aware of the presence of your angels and deceased loved ones, you'll enjoy being with them, and you'll benefit from them more.

If you want to have contact with your angels, deceased loved ones, or an ascended master, these next few chapters will describe some methods that can help you. These are the same techniques that I teach my psychic-development students, and they're also the same ones that I use myself before I give readings. They're very powerful.

Most people have some ambivalence about contacting heavenly beings. On the one hand, they desperately want to see an angel or departed loved one. But they also fear seeing a frightening image. "Will I be opening myself up to seeing dark beings? Or will my deceased loved one look ghoulish?" These are natural concerns, as people worry about losing control, or being frightened out of their wits.

So, one of my wishes is that the stories related in this book will boost your confidence that heavenly encounters are positive, happy experiences. Know that you won't see upsetting images when your angels and deceased loved ones pay you a visit.

While it's true that there are "unsavory" beings in heaven, they are a slim minority compared to all the magnificent angels and guides constantly flitting around us on the etheric plane.

One of the greatest angels of all, Archangel Michael, can prevent you from having a frightening encounter. All you need to do is mentally say to him:

"Archangel Michael, please escort away from me anyone who is not my angel, guide, or a being who expresses God's Divine light."

Michael needs to receive this sort of explicit request because God's Law of Free Will prevents him from helping us unless we ask.

Archangel Michael is able to be with everyone simultaneously who calls upon him, and there are no time or space restraints. So it's a good idea to ask him to stay permanently stationed by your side. Ask him to screen the beings in your life—both the physical and the spiritual ones—so that only benevolent entities surround you. Once you've asked Michael for help, you can relax. This request is always granted for everyone, regardless of lifestyle, religion, or character. So don't worry that your requests might be denied. They can't be!

It's important to clear fears out of the way, because they can prevent you from having a heavenly encounter. Ambivalent people are putting one foot on the gas pedal and one on the brakes simultaneously, which keeps them from moving forward.

Trying Too Hard

Another issue that prevents people from seeing their angels and deceased loved ones is the fear of failure. This fear often makes people push and strain to have an angel encounter. They try to force it to happen, which blocks the experience completely. The sad irony is that the people who love angels the most are often the ones who have the hardest time seeing them!

At almost every one of my workshops, I see the following scenario played out: An angel-loving woman will arrive, accompanied by her loyal husband. She's dressed in an angel sweatshirt, angel earrings, and an angel necklace. He really could care less about angels but is just coming to the workshop to please his wife.

Then the workshop begins, and before lunchtime, I've guided the audience through an exercise that helps them see angels. The husband is seeing angels and deceased loved ones, and he says to his wife, "Wow, honey, this is amazing! Thanks for bringing me to this conference." She, meanwhile, has had no success at seeing any heavenly beings, and she snaps at him, "How come *you're* seeing angels? You don't even like them!"

Her frustration stems from her underlying belief that since she's a member of the angel "fan club," she's entitled to insider privileges. But the angels are equally devoted to all of us, even to nonbelievers and newcomers. Her main block has to do with the fact that she desperately wants to see angels, so she's trying too hard to make it happen. Her husband, who has a nonchalant attitude about heaven, is relaxed and more open to the experience. One such husband recently completed my Angel Therapy Practitioner certification course, and he's now a professional angel reader. Yet he was originally a "drag-along" at one of my workshops a couple of years ago.

So, straining and pushing can actually prevent us from connecting with our angels. The fear that causes us to force things to happen comes from feeling alone, and the belief that "if it's going to be, it's up to me." However, our angel encounters are derived from the power of God, the angels, ascended masters, and our deceased loved ones. A teamwork approach to angel encounters works best.

Clearing the Fear

In addition to calling upon Archangel Michael, here are two other ways to diminish or eliminate fear blocks:

1. The freezer method. Write your fears on a piece of paper. You can either include an elaborate description of your fears, or just a general "fear of being psychic" sentence. Then, put the paper into your refrigerator's freezer compartment. If you live with skeptics, it's best to put the paper in the back of the freezer, where it will be unnoticed, or freeze it in a small container of water. Leave the paper in the freezer for a minimum of three months. This method also works well with anything in your life that you'd like to release, including problems with relationships, addictions, or money issues.

2. The dream method. The angels do some of their best work while we're sleeping. Why? Because our fears are asleep at that time, so we're more open to angelic assistance. Before you go to sleep at night, mentally ask Archangel Michael, Archangel Raphael (who's in charge of physical healings), and Archangel Uriel (whose area is emotional and psychological healings) to enter your dreams. Mentally say to them:

"Please enter my dream, my body, my mind, and my heart; and clear away any fears or unforgiveness that could be blocking me from having a conscious angel encounter."

Intention Is Everything

The angels have a phrase that they love to repeat: "Your intentions create your experiences." This means that our underlying expectations steer us toward the type of experiences we have as a result. If we hold positive expectations about our angel encounters, we'll have positive results.

However, if we have negative intentions, such as, *Gee, I sure hope I can do this,* or *I'm afraid to see the spirit world,* or *Will God punish me for doing this?* then we will be blocked from having an angel encounter. For one thing, the angels love us deeply, and they wouldn't do anything to frighten us, such as showing up if we don't really want to see them. The same goes for your deceased loved ones. Your grandparents, mom, dad, siblings, or other loved ones see your fear as a giant KEEP AWAY! sign. They will respect that boundary out of love.

"I really want to see my mom, but I'm afraid that she'll have Aunt Edna with her. And I don't want any contact with Aunt Edna!" said Betsy, a woman at one of my seminars. She explained that her aunt had been bossy and verbally abusive. Betsy was afraid that by seeing her mother, she'd be opening the gates of heaven so that other "less desirable" relatives would show up uninvited. This is another area to delegate to Archangel Michael, who's happy to act as your "bouncer" angel. He'll screen your visitors, if you just ask him to.

One of the reasons why children are so psychic is because of their positive intentions. They don't worry, *Am I making this up, or is it real?* Children know that reality comes in many flavors. They also trust their intuition to a higher degree than most adults. Additionally, their lives are simpler than adults', in general, so their minds are less cluttered with distractions, worries, pressure, and noise.

So, to open yourself to an encounter with heaven, be "as a little child." Let go of rigid expectations about your angel connection. Just hold a positive intention such as, *I'd really like to meet my guardian angel,* or *I would love to see and talk with Mom,* and then release the desire to the winds of the universe. Trust your angels to catch your wish and bring it to you in a delightfully surprising way.

That's why it's important not to dictate to God how you want your angel encounter to manifest. For instance, don't say to the angels, "Please brush my hair as a sign that you're with me." Instead, simply say, "Please give me a sign that you're with me," and let them figure out the best method for delivering that request. Remind yourself frequently that the "how" of the way prayers are answered is up to God, not up to us. The infinite creativity of the Divine Mind is filled with happy surprises that defy the physical laws of Earth, which our human minds often worry about.

So, holding positive intentions is essential. Even if you don't fully believe in angel encounters because you haven't yet experienced one firsthand, hold a positive intention. Even if you're not sure if you're qualified or deserving of an angel encounter (which I assure you that you *are!*), hold a positive intention. Even if you want to see an angel or deceased loved one so badly that it hurts, hold a positive intention.

Here are some affirmations to help you elevate your intentions to the most positive and optimistic level possible. Read, write, or say these affirmations as often as possible:

- *I feel safe in opening my psychic abilities.*

- *I am highly visual.*

- *I am very clairvoyant.*

- *I easily hear the voice of God and the angels.*

- *I am open to seeing my deceased loved ones.*

- *I welcome my angels into my dreams.*

- *God and the angels love me very much.*

- *I can feel the presence of angels around me right now.*

- *God and the angels speak to me continually.*

- *I notice signs from heaven.*

- *I am open to Divine communication.*

- *I trust God to protect me.*

ANSWERED PRAYERS

The Law of Free Will says that heaven cannot intervene or interfere in our lives unless we give our permission. The only exception is to save our lives—if it isn't our time yet to go. So, you'll need to request that your angels help you to clearly see, hear, or feel their presence. There are many ways to do so, including the following:

— **Praying.** State your request to God and the angels. For example, "God, I deeply desire to meet my guardian angel. Please help me see and hear this angel." Say this prayer repeatedly until you feel a sense of peace and inevitability in your heart and gut area.

— **Directly asking.** Many people encounter a deceased loved one directly after asking that person for help. You can do so aloud, in written form, or silently. Let's say that you're worried about a particular deceased loved one. Ask that person for some sort of reassurance that everything is okay. That person will then contact you, either through a dream visitation, in an apparition encounter, or by giving you a sign. If your experience isn't clear enough for you, then ask the person for additional contact.

— **Writing a letter.** This technique works best when conducted in an isolated environment. So, go find a quiet place outdoors, or sequester yourself in your corner of the house (including the bathroom, if there's no other private place!). Write a letter to God, your guardian angels, or your deceased loved one. Pour your heart out about your desire for an angel encounter, and your fears or reservations. End the letter with a strong request for their help.

— **Using possessions.** Kirlian photography shows that an object's aura is affected by the emotions of the person who held it. In other words, people's energy is imprinted upon their possessions. As a result, you can tune in to your deceased loved one by holding one of his or her possessions in the hand you normally don't write with (that is, your energy-receiving hand). It's best to hold an object that your loved one came into constant contact with—for instance, a ring, watch, eyeglasses, or a necklace. Metal items hold the energy best, but any object will do in a pinch. You can also hold a person's photograph as a way of tuning in to his or her energy.

As you hold the object, close your eyes and hold the intention of psychically connecting with that person. Ask your angels to act as telephone operators, routing your call. Whether you feel your loved one's presence or not, mentally ask the person to contact you.

— **Going outside in nature.** Perhaps the reason why so many people have encounters with their deceased loved ones at grave sites is because they're outdoors. Souls certainly don't hang around where their bones are buried or their ashes are contained. After death, we no longer identify with our physical bodies! However, when you visit a deceased loved one's grave, you're thinking about the person strongly, and you're outside in nature. You can replicate those same two conditions (without visiting the grave) in order to make contact. Simply go to a beautiful place in nature, and hold strong thoughts about your loved one.

This works especially well if you go to a place that reminds you of the departed. For instance, if your deceased loved one was fanatical about the mountains, you might connect more deeply after you hike partway up one. Or, if the two of you loved strolling around the local lake, visit this location and hold the intention of contacting your departed one. As you walk lakeside, imagine that your loved one is beside you, and have a mental conversation. Before long, you'll probably realize that your loved one *is* there and that your conversation is real!

— **Holding a ceremony.** Just because your loved one's body is gone doesn't mean that you can't celebrate a birthday or other significant date. After my Grandma Pearl passed away, I held a birthday "party" in her honor, complete with a huge bouquet of her favorite flowers (gladiolas) gracing the table. She definitely attended, enjoyed, and appreciated this ceremony from the spirit world.

Your departed family members attend every significant ceremony and get-together that you hold, so don't ignore them! Mentally or verbally say hello to your deceased loved ones whenever you hold a family gathering. They will appreciate being recognized and remembered; and you're more likely to see, hear, or feel their presence.

You can also hold a ceremony in order to contact your guardian angels or ascended masters. For instance, on holidays in Jesus's honor, you might feel especially open and close to him, which could spark an encounter. Or you can create a ceremony to contact your angels and guides, using free-form dance or drumming.

With positive optimism, you will be more open to the angel experiences that are occurring around you continually. Just be open and aware. Your angel connection will most likely happen when you least expect it, since that's when you're most relaxed and open.

As this book demonstrates, heavenly encounters can take a variety of forms. Apparition experiences, dream visitations, disembodied voices, encounters with a mysterious stranger, or other signs are just a few of the ways that heaven will answer your prayers.

∾ ∾ ∾

Chapter 16

A One-Week Plan to Open Yourself to Angel Visions

This chapter outlines a powerful plan of action that can give you the maximum opportunity to see angels. For some of you, the results will be immediate, and you may see angels or your deceased loved one right away. Others may need to be more patient, and it could be several weeks before you have angel visions. However, if you follow these steps, you'll definitely have breakthroughs that will lead you toward these sightings. I'm asking you to perform these steps every day for seven days. As soon as you're ready to see angels, they will appear.

You probably noticed that a common thread among the stories of people who saw their deceased loved one in a dream or as an apparition was that the person was in a state of crisis, or had a strong emotional need to connect with the loved one. When you deeply long for certain individuals, a signal is emitted to heaven. Those above know that you strongly desire a conversation. In fact, your loved one has probably already visited you. If you thought you "felt" his or her presence, you were most likely correct. You didn't see the person or you don't remember your dream interactions because of your heightened emotional state of grief, fear, or anger.

If you've been afraid to see an apparition, your deceased loved one won't appear to you because he or she loves you and doesn't want to scare you. However, if you've honestly faced your fears and taken spiritual or psychological steps to heal those fears, the departed spirit is more likely to appear to you now.

There is never a guarantee that the person will appear to you, and if you don't see him or her, it's important not to let yourself get upset. It doesn't mean that your deceased loved one is mad at you or doesn't love you just because you haven't seen him or her. If someone else in your family *has* seen the individual in question, it's not a sign of favoritism—it just means that the other person was more "ready" to see an apparition than you were.

It takes a lot of energy for a person in the spirit world to appear in apparition form, similar to how it feels when we dive to the deepest ocean floor. Sometimes deceased loved ones have to "borrow" a charge from the "battery" of their own spirit guides to have enough energy to glow visibly for the living. One study of individuals who had seen apparitions from their deathbed found that the vast majority only saw their deceased loved ones for five minutes or less.[1] The spirit world can often only sustain an apparition appearance for brief periods of time. So, I don't want you to expect to spend hours and hours conversing with your deceased loved one. Some people do, but usually you'll see and talk to the person from the spirit world rather briefly. Yet even though it's a short visit, you'll likely find it life changing and highly therapeutic.

Your visit with a guardian angel of the winged variety, or with a spirit guide who glows so bright that you may not even see his or her facial features, might also be brief. In such encounters, though, you'll have a feeling of time standing still. So afterward, it may be difficult for you to calculate how long your angel encounter lasted.

---

[1]   Osis, K., and Haraldsson, E. 1997. *At the Hour of Death.* Third Edition (Norwalk, CT: Hastings House).

Seven-Day Plan for Having an Angel Vision

Here are the steps that I teach the students in my mediumship, psychic-development, and clairvoyance classes. Usually I suggest that people try one or two of these steps at a time, but I understand that you're very serious about seeing an angel or a deceased loved one, so I'm going to ask you to go into heavy-duty training, and undertake all of the steps in sequence. Just keep going through the days until you have your breakthrough vision.

As I said earlier, it might happen on day 2 or on day 42. But one thing's for sure: if you follow these steps as prescribed, you will eventually have visions. Your determination in adhering to the steps is up to you. If this process is truly important to you, then please perform these steps as long as is necessary. As an added benefit, you may also find that they help you feel lighter, happier, stronger, and healthier.

First, choose a day to begin, and write it on your calendar as "The Beginning of Angel Visions." The day before you're scheduled to begin, you'll need to stock up on some earthly supplies and shop for foods that will enhance your psychic abilities. Go to a health-food store, if possible, for these items. Or, find a local fruit stand or a grocery store with superior produce.

Buy yourself several types of fresh fruit, preferably organic. In sequential order of their ability to support your psychic abilities, purchase: fresh pineapple, grapefruit, oranges, apples, lemons, berries, and melons. Then, purchase some organic, whole-grain breakfast cereal; whole-grain rice; mixed salad greens; natural salad dressing (without chemical ingredients); raw nuts; hummus; and some meat replacements such as tofu, seitan, and veggie burgers, or look through your health-food store's deli and frozen-food section for various meat substitutes. While you're at it, buy one or two vegetarian cookbooks, or *Vegetarian Times* magazine, to guide you through the ins and outs of this eating style.

Maintaining a vegetarian diet is the quickest route to developing clairvoyance. Even quicker is a "vegan" diet, which means that you avoid all meat, fowl, fish, or dairy products, and use meat substitutes and soy milk products. In fact, dairy products, red meat, chocolate, and alcohol are the greatest blocks to clairvoyance. For further explanation of the link between diet and psychic abilities, please see my books *The Art of Raw Living Food* (co-authored with Jenny Ross), *Chakra Clearing,* and *Divine Prescriptions.*

Note: Each morning's activities will take at least 20 minutes, so you may need to adjust your routine and set your alarm clock 20 minutes earlier than normal. Some of the activities may seem odd to you, and you may wonder if you could skip some of them. My advice to you is to perform them all; and if you feel uncomfortable about any of them, ask God and your angels to help ease your discomfort or give you a substitute activity. The first day, you may feel overwhelmed by all that I'm asking you to do, but you'll soon develop a routine that will take less effort. Besides, any extra effort will be worth it, and you'll find that you have more energy throughout the day as a result.

What to Do Each Day

1. Morning meditation. Immediately after waking up and taking your morning bathroom break, engage in meditation before taking part in any lengthy conversation with family members or roommates. Each day, there's a different morning and evening meditation to focus upon. You can combine this with your other regular meditation practices, or use it solo.

2. Journal. Next, write (on a notepad or in a formal journal or diary) a letter to whomever you want to see. It could be a carte blanche letter to "Whoever is my guardian angel," to a specific deceased loved one, to Jesus or a saint, or to God asking to see whom you're supposed to see. Your letter needs to be from your heart, where you pour out your feelings. Remember that all of the stories in this book have shown the correlation between a person having strong emotions and then later seeing a deceased loved one or angels. So, let your feelings out in your letter! Don't worry about grammar, spelling, or proper syntax. Just write from the heart.

3. Chant. In this next step (you may need to go outside to do this and the following step), you will use the ancient science called "toning" to open up your third eye. Chant the sound of God or Creation seven times, preferably out loud. If your family is skeptical, you can chant quietly, but in general the louder, the better. If you have reservations about chanting, or fears that this may be a spooky occult practice, please read the section at the end of this chapter entitled "About Chanting." You'll read one woman's remarkable story of having an angel vision after she began this practice.

Close your eyes and say "Aaaahhhh, Uuuuhhhh, Mmmm" seven times. While you're chanting, place your focus on the area between your two physical eyes, and hold the positive thought, *It is safe for me to see angels.* Concentrate on seeing whoever it is you want to see. If you have any negative or frightening thoughts, please don't fight them. Instead, mentally ask your angels to take the thoughts away.

4. Spin. After you have chanted the AUM sound seven times, stand up and spread your arms straight out from your sides. With your eyes open, find an item or a shape on the wall, a nearby tree, a curtain, or some other interesting eye-level object. This is your "visual anchor." Then look at that object and slowly spin your body to the right (clockwise). Your body will get to an angle where you can no longer see your visual anchor. Just keep spinning clockwise, and turn your head to the left to spot your visual anchor again, and guide your body back to face the visual anchor.

Do this spinning exercise three times each morning. If you feel dizzy, it means that your third-eye chakra (the window of clairvoyance) is dirty. As you cleanse your chakra through meditation, chanting, light eating, and spinning, you'll be able to rotate more times without feeling dizzy. For now, though, spin slowly during each rotation. You can also stop at the end of the three spins and put your hands in a prayer position (or "Namaste" position) in front of your chest as a way to stop the dizziness.

5. Eat in the light. You should eat a vegetarian or vegan diet (no meat or dairy) to the extent that you want to have angel visions. In other words, the more vegetarian foods that you can eat, the more readily your angel visions will come. So, a 70 percent vegetarian diet would yield a 70 percent chance of seeing an angel or deceased loved one, and so on.

In addition, mentally ask your angels to heal any cravings you may have for the two substances that block psychic abilities the most: alcohol and chocolate. If you're really serious and sincere about seeing angels, you'll abstain from these two things for now. The angels can release you from *desiring* alcohol or chocolate so that you won't feel deprived. Just ask for their help by saying something such as:

"Angels, I want to see you, so I ask you to enter my body, mind, and heart, and heal away any fears or sense of emptiness that leads me to crave mood-altering food or drinks. I am willing to release the need to eat chocolate or drink alcohol. I know that these substances are poor substitutes for Divine love and energy. Thank you, and amen."

In addition, keep your caffeine, sugar, nicotine, and processed-food intake to a minimum during this seven-day period. Instead, drink plenty of room-temperature spring or artesian water (not sparkling, purified, distilled, or tap water); or rainwater that you catch in bowls during a rainstorm. Or, drink freshly squeezed citrus juice, especially if it comes from organic produce. You'll find that natural water and fresh, organic juices boost your energy much more than any caffeinated beverage.

6. Nature time. Five minutes a day, take off your shoes, socks, or nylons, and stand with your bare feet on Mother Earth. Let your flesh connect with soil, grass, or sand. You and the earth need to touch each other in a "mystical meeting" to psychically exchange vital information—as well as playful love—with one another. By keeping this Divine daily appointment with your Mother, you will feel more of a kinship with all of life. And part of opening your psychic visions is knowing that you are one with everyone and everything.

In addition, make sure that you're surrounded by healthy, live plants in your home and office. Plants absorb the energy of our fear and stress in the same way that they absorb carbon dioxide. It is especially important to sleep next to a live plant. The broad-leafed varieties, such as pothos or philodendrons, are best at absorbing negative energy.

7. Exercise. Every day, engage in some sort of heart-opening physical activity, such as yoga, brisk walking, running, swimming, biking, or any other exercise that elevates your pulse for at least 30 minutes. Aerobic exercise clears away fear's toxic residue, which builds up in the body.

8. Evening chant. Chant "AUM" seven times, as discussed in Step 3.

9. Evening meditation. Spend at least ten minutes alone, even if you have to lock yourself in the bathroom, and take several deep breaths. Focus on the evening meditation corresponding to the particular day of your seven-day plan.

10. Evening angel discussion. As you fall asleep, mentally talk to your angel or deceased loved one. Pour your heart out about your feelings, about what happened to you during the day, and any issue that you need assistance with. Ask your angel or deceased loved one to enter your dreams or visibly appear to you. Ask for help in losing your fears so that you can stay calm and centered. Ask for help, also, to remember any dream encounter that you may have with your angel or deceased loved one (although most such encounters are so vivid that they are unforgettable).

Morning and Evening Meditations

Day 1—Morning:

"I now feel myself surrounded by the healing presence of my angels. I feel their wings enfolding me, helping me to know that I am safe and eternally loved. As I breathe in and out, I feel their unconditional love for me as warmth in my chest and heart. I allow myself to feel loved, knowing that it is safe to open my heart to Divine caring."

Day 1—Evening:

"I know that I am safe, continuously guarded by large angels who watch over me. I know that God's infinite wisdom and unconditional love are supporting me right now. I ask for [name of whoever it is you would like to see] *to appear to me visually. I know that it is safe for me to see. I do not strain or push, but I now allow visions to come to me at a pace that I can easily handle."*

&⁊⁊

Day 2—Morning:

"Everything is in Divine and perfect order, right now. I see angels in God's perfect timing, and I release any need to rush my angel visions. As I breathe in and out, I release any old toxins in my body related to fears about opening myself up to psychic visions. I release toxins related to any past experience that was painful. [Breathe in and out deeply.] *I let everything go. I now see a golden light inside my head. I see that golden light forming a rope, and I feel that rope moving from inside my head out into the room, like a pipe cleaner. I now feel my third eye being cleansed by the light of my Holy Spirit. I allow Spirit to cleanse and open me to Divine experiences, now."*

Day 2—Evening:

"I breathe in deeply, drawing in the life force energy of the world. I am one with this energy. My angels and deceased loved ones are one with this energy. As I exhale completely, I breathe out all stress, doubt, and fear completely. I now breathe in deeply, drawing in faith, confidence, and knowingness. I exhale skepticism. I inhale acceptance. I exhale fear. I inhale faith. I exhale everything that I do not want in my life. I inhale everything that I desire. I exhale anger. I inhale gratitude."

❧❧

Day 3—Morning:

"Dear God and Holy Spirit, I deeply desire to see my angel [or name of deceased loved one]. *I ask Your help in bringing this about. Please give me clear Divine guidance that I will easily understand to help me know what to do in order to have an angel vision. Please help me lose any fears that may be blocking my spiritual sight. Please help me see Your miraculous angels."*

Day 3—Evening:

"I now ask my angels and [name of deceased loved one and/or ascended master whom you would like to see] *to enter my dreams. My heart and mind are open to all possibilities, and I am ready to receive love and truth. I know that I am safe in having angel visions, and I affirm that Divine love encircles me now. It is safe for me to see angels. It is safe for me to see truth. It is safe for me to see the future. It is safe for me to see."*

❧❧

Day 4—Morning:

"My spiritual sight is now wide-open, and all around me is incredible beauty. Everywhere I look, I see evidence of love. I see loving actions, the exquisiteness of nature, and the attractiveness of everyone and everything. As I see only love, then only love can come into my awareness. I now see love in the embodiment of angels."

Day 4—Evening:

"I ask for Archangel Michael to enter my dreams tonight and clear away any fears that could be keeping me from having full faith. I now allow God's Divine love to expand throughout my being, filling me with eternal confidence and eradicating any illusions of fear. I am safe, and I am loved."

❧❧

Day 5—Morning:

"Today I see the glowing lights of angels that constantly surround every person. I see glowing shades of white, gold, green, blue, and purple around everyone's head and shoulders. I easily connect with this angel energy, and I receive Divine messages throughout the day. These messages always speak of Divine love and selfless service, and help me stay centered in an awareness of my gratitude for heaven upon Earth."

Day 5—Evening:

"I allow goodness to come to me without forcing or chasing anything. I know that forcing anything to happen comes from an underlying thought of fear. I know that fear blocks the very experiences I desire. I completely surrender my desire to have an angel vision. I trust God and heaven to bring my heart's desire to me. My only task is to open the door, by surrendering all forms of fear. The rest will happen naturally."

∽∾

Day 6—Morning:

"Today I intend to have a happy day. I ask God and my angels to guide me so that I may feel happiness throughout the day. I ask to bring blessings to everyone who sees, meets, or thinks of me today. I ask to be an earth angel today."

Day 6—Evening:

"Dear Angel [or name of the being whom you would like to see], *I deeply desire to see you. Please enter my dreams, or manifest into a visible apparition so that I may see and experience you without delay. I ask that you allow me to see you. If I am blocking this experience in any way, please give me a strong and unmistakable message so that I may have clear spiritual sight."*

∽∾

Day 7—Morning:

"As I tune in to my third eye, I am aware of sparkling white, blue, and purple light. [Please take a moment to close your physical eyes and see these colors right in front of you.] *I now ask for Archangel Raphael to place his index finger on my third eye, and heal away any last remaining vestiges of fear that may be covering my spiritual vision. I trust that my veil has lifted and that I now can see clearly. I am ready to see now!"*

Day 7—Evening:
"I am now aware of the presence of my guardian angels. As I breathe in and out, I relax and attune to the awareness of them. I allow myself to feel the depth of their love for me. I feel their warmth. I feel their unconditional love. I am one with my angels. I am one with love. I now give myself permission to visually connect with my angels."

ABOUT CHANTING

To some, the idea of chanting may seem unnatural or uncomfortable, yet it is an ancient technique for achieving spiritual visions. Far from being an occult practice, chanting stems from affirming the holy name of our Creator. When chanting the word *Aum,* you are actually singing a love song to God. *Aum* is actually the root of the word *Amen,* which closes most Christian prayers.

Here is a story of a woman who was able to have an angel vision, thanks to the help that chanting gave her.

HOW CHANTING HELPED ME SEE MY ANGEL
by Molly Donohue

On Christmas Day, 1999, I saw an angel floating above my bed. While I was reading Doreen's book *Divine Guidance,* I said a prayer that I would actually like to see one of my angels. I had been following Doreen's advice about chanting "Aaaahhhh, Uuuuhhhh, Mmmm" seven times every morning and every night for about a week.

In the middle of the night, I was woken up by the sight of a bright reddish-white light. The sight was strange, as if there was a planetarium above my bed. The brilliance of the light dimmed somewhat, and I saw a beautiful female angel lying on her side, looking down at me.

Of course I was startled, but soon after, I was filled with a feeling of warmth and love, and I simply wasn't scared anymore. I remembered reading in Doreen's book that angels are messengers, so I asked what her name was and what message she had for me.

Telepathically, she said that her name was Annabelle. She looked just like the angels in Renaissance paintings, and her message was simple. She wanted me to know that I was supremely loved, more than I could even imagine. She wanted me to know that I was watched every moment, and a legion of angels and guides awaited my requests. I asked her about a book I thought I was supposed to write. She confirmed that it was Divine guidance for me to write it, but that was not her role.

She was sent in answer to a prayer, and to express love—Divine love. I basked in the love and radiance for at least 30 minutes. I even went to the bathroom during that time, and she was still there when I came back out, just radiating love and light. Then she slowly faded out, back to just reddish white, then to nothingness. It was one of the most wonderful experiences of my life. I now continue to see, hear, and feel my angels all the time.

∞ ∞ ∞

Chapter 17

How to See an Angel

If you follow the seven-day plan from Chapter 16, continue repeating the process for as many days as it takes, and if you're truly ready to see an angel, there's no reason why you won't have an angel vision. The methods outlined in the previous chapter are all powerful, time-honored steps that lead to visions. They work . . . if you commit to practicing them consistently.

As you've read in the stories in this book, different people have different ways of seeing their angels. Yet, whether their experience involved a dream, a waking state, seeing lights, or having a helpful encounter with a mysterious stranger, the authors of the stories you've read about have one thing in common: their angel vision was deeply meaningful and life changing.

You probably have a preference regarding the way you'd like to see your angels (and in this chapter, I'm using the word *angel* to collectively mean an angel with wings, a deceased loved one, or an ascended master), yet your angel vision will occur exactly in the manner that you're most ready for. If you would be frightened by seeing a big beautiful angel in your living room, then your angel vision will occur as a dream or in the form of seeing lights.

In my workshops, I find that my audience members experience angel visions in many different ways, including seeing an angel . . .

- • . . . with their physical eyes open.

- • . . . in their mind's eye, with their physical eyes shut.

- • . . . as a partial picture in their mind's eye.

Some of my audience members experience angel visions that look like wispy, smokelike images. Others see angels that are more opaque and solid looking. Some people see angels in their mind's eye that look like they are stationed over other people. To others, the angels that they see in their mind's eye seem to be located inside their own head.

When I see angels, I typically have my eyes open. When I was a child, I couldn't distinguish deceased people from the living. Now that I'm older, my angel visions are less opaque. The angels I see remind me of the experience of being in a living room with friends, with the TV set on. I can see both the people who are physically present with me, as well as the people on TV. I know that those who are on the screen are not as "real" as those who are sitting on the sofa next to me.

So, your angel visions will probably have a different quality from seeing a living person. Nonetheless, you will know that you are interacting with a sentient being who is quite alive. You won't have much doubt, if any, whether your experience is real. In most angel visions, you'll receive a message from the angel that will be wordlessly transferred into your heart or your mind. You'll "know" or "feel" exactly what the angel is telling you.

> ## Please Don't Strain!
>
> You'll block your angel visions if you try too hard.
>
> *Do* pray hard to see your angel and release your fears that could block angel visions.
>
> Please don't force the experience to happen.
>
> Let the angel visions come to you.
>
> Imagine that you are a satellite dish that receives signals.

DIFFERENT WAYS TO SEE ANGELS

After following the seven-day plan, and repeating it if necessary, you'll probably have a spontaneous angel vision. Most likely, it will happen when you least expect it. For instance, you'll awaken in the middle of the night and see an angel standing near the foot of the bed. The incredible love permeating from the angel will allay any fears that you'd normally have. Or, you'll be driving and spontaneously see an angel hovering over the hood of your car. The possibilities for your out-of-the-blue angel vision are endless.

While going through these exercises, it's vital to hold positive expectations that you will see angels! So, if you're holding negative intentions toward angel visions such as, *Gee, I hope I can really do this,* or *I'm kind of doubtful that I'm qualified to see angels,* you'll be blocked because you *expect* to be blocked.

Doubts are normal from time to time. The key is to be aware of these negative intentions, and then to mentally ask your angels to help remove these thoughts and feelings and their residue. Before you begin these exercises, take a few moments to close your eyes, breathe deeply, and see or feel eight glass globes stacked on top of each other. From top to bottom, the colors of the globes are:

- Purple
- Red violet
- Deep blue
- Light blue
- Emerald green

- Yellow

- Orange

- Red

See or feel these globes as brightly colored, and free of any spots or dirt. Picture a bright white light illuminating the interior of each globe.

Then mentally affirm:

I now easily see the spirit world.

*I am a powerful clairvoyant who uses my gift in
beautiful service to the world.*

It is safe for me to see.

I am surrounded by security, protection, and quiet peacefulness.

Partner Exercises

In each partner exercise, you'll want to work with someone who is open-minded and who believes in angels (or who would like to believe in angels). Although it is very possible to gain important angelic experiences while working with skeptics, their negative mindset toward life after death and angels could frustrate you in your initial attempts at seeing angels. So, please select your most faith-filled friend or family member.

Wall Work

Ask your friend to stand against a plain white wall. The wall should have a minimum of texture and no wallpaper. A solid white screen, used for movie projection, works wonderfully well, also.

Ask your friend to close his or her eyes so that you don't feel any sense of pressure or awkwardness as you conduct this exercise. Then, take a few deep breaths, and squint your eyes slightly. Soften your gaze, as if you're looking past your friend.

With your softened focus, scan around your friend's head and shoulders. Don't strain to see anything; let the visual awareness come to you naturally. Notice if you see or sense any white light, or other colors glowing around your partner. Perhaps you see waves of energy, similar to seeing heat waves emanating from the street on a hot day.

Then, take another deep breath and close your eyes. Compare what you see around your friend's head and shoulders once you close your eyes (some people see the spirit world more easily if they shut their eyes). If you "see" more easily with your physical eyes closed, then please keep them shut throughout the rest of this exercise. However, you may see the energy or light of the angels more readily with your eyes open; and if so, please keep your physical eyes open during the exercise.

Once you see any sort of light, bump, or other indication of a presence, keep breathing in and out as your spiritual sight adjusts to seeing. Just like when you exit a dark movie theater during the day, your eyes will need some time to adjust, and focus on what they are seeing. Don't worry whether this is your imagination or not; just keep noticing any details about the angels around your partner.

Pairing Work

This is an exercise designed so that both partners can simultaneously have an angel vision. First, sit facing your friend. Hold hands, and both of you should have your eyes closed. Rest your hands in a comfortable place, such as one person's lap, so that they don't get tired. Breathe in and out regularly. (We sometimes hold our breath when we're under pressure.) Breathing opens up the psychic senses. Also, take your time with this exercise, since any sense of time urgency could block you.

Now, imagine what it would be like if you could see your partner's guardian angels. Just give yourself permission to imagine seeing your friend's angels. It doesn't matter whether you're making this up or are really seeing those angels. Just let yourself see them.

What do they look like? Are they tall or short? Do they seem female, male, or androgynous? What color are their eyes? What is the style and color of their hair? Do you see any wings? Any other details about them? Do you have a sense of any message that the angels are sending your partner?

After a few minutes of seeing the angels around your partner, go ahead and tell him or her everything that you saw, felt, heard, or thought. Don't worry whether it was "real" or not. One of the reasons why children are so highly psychic is that they are unconcerned with differentiating between mere imagination and true reality. Our guardedness as adults is one of the chief blocks that keeps us from seeing beyond the veil. The irony is that when you let down any defensiveness against mistaking fantasy for reality, you'll have your real angel-vision breakthroughs.

You will know or feel the reality of your vision, and your partner will validate that the vision rings true for him or her. However, if you doubt whether you really saw an angel, be sure to ask God and the angels to guide you to a true angel vision, or to help you release any erroneous doubts that keep you from enjoying your angel visions.

There is no limit to the number of times you can see your winged guardian angels or someone such as Jesus, Yogananda, or a saint. However, your recently deceased loved one may not be able to visually appear to you frequently. It takes a tremendous amount of energy for a deceased person to appear in apparition form, so you may only see your deceased loved one once a month, for instance. After all, newly deceased people can't stay on the Earth-plane level continuously. They've got heavenly growth work to do before they can be assigned as someone's permanent spirit guide. But after tuning in to him or her visually, you will be able to sense and feel the person's presence more readily. And be assured that your deceased loved one always hears your prayers, messages, requests, and questions. The departed are never out of earshot, and when you call upon them, they are with you as soon as they possibly can be.

SOLO EXERCISES

Appointment with an Angel

Decide which heavenly being you would like to see. It could be a deceased loved one or your winged guardian angel, for example. Then, get out your calendar and choose a day and time when you'll have at least two uninterrupted hours alone. Mark on your calendar "My appointment with an angel."

Then, go somewhere alone, such as a bathroom, your backyard or patio, or your meditation area. Close your physical eyes and focus on the heavenly being you would like to see. Mentally call to this being. Send the being love energy from your heart and belly.

Then, mentally explain to the being that you would like to meet with him or her (give the exact day and time of your appointment). If you get a strong feeling that this doesn't work for your angel or deceased loved one, then you may need to choose a different appointment time. It could be that your angel knows this won't be an optimal moment for your connection (such as the angel foreseeing an unscheduled activity that would interrupt you), or your deceased loved one may have a prior obligation (such as performing service work, which most people do in heaven).

Once you feel a sense of peace about your appointment time, mentally tell the being about the physical location where you plan to be. You are doing this for *your* sake, not for the heavenly being (he or she can find you quite easily, no matter where you are). The point is to have a clear mental image of your forthcoming appointment. See yourself connecting, and hold a positive expectation that you will have some breakthroughs with your angel vision. Remember, your intentions create your experience. So, hold an optimistic intention, without any sense of strain or urgency.

It's vital that you keep your appointment. If you truly can't do so or if you need to select a new location, then mentally reschedule with your angel.

On the day of your appointment, arrive punctually with a pad of paper and a medium-point pen. Sit down and mentally greet your angel or deceased loved one. Close your eyes and breathe, noticing the feeling that the being is with you. Mentally greet the being, and begin having a mental conversation. Let the answers come to you as feelings, words, thoughts, or visions.

Say a prayer for God's Divine light to surround you. Mentally ask Archangel Michael to stay next to you during your appointment to ensure that only your angel or invited deceased loved one comes to you.

Then, open your eyes and write on the paper: "How can I see you?" Think the question as you write it. Jot down whatever impressions come to you, even if you seem to be receiving nothing. Automatic writing sometimes begins as a small trickle, but if you'll just scribble anything that pops into your mind, you'll start opening the floodgates. Keep going by writing other questions you think of, and then recording the impressions that come to you in response. Before long, you'll really be having conversations with heaven.

Your heavenly being will give you very helpful suggestions that will assist you in having angel visions. You may receive guidance to make lifestyle changes, meditate more often, or reframe your beliefs. By following this step-by-step guidance, you'll be on your way to having angel visions. However, it is also very likely that you'll actually see your angel or deceased loved one during your appointment. Either way, keep going, and with practice and patience, you'll be having helpful and loving conversations with heaven regularly.

Mirror Work

For this exercise, you'll need a dimly lit room with a large mirror. You can do this exercise in the evening, using a nightlight. But many people find it frightening to look in a mirror in the dark, so it's better to be in a diffuse-light room during the day. So, cover your bathroom window with a thick towel, for instance.

Stand in front of the mirror and smile. When you do so, you'll automatically relax and make the exercise a more pleasant experience, instead of an intense or frightening one. You might even make funny faces in the mirror so that you'll laugh and relax even more.

A secret to having angel visions is to be at ease and have fun during the entire process.

Then, with an "easy does it," nonchalant attitude, gaze into the mirror at yourself, and scan around your head and shoulders. Don't try to force your angel vision; just allow anything that comes to you to be a pleasant surprise. You may see a glowing aura around your head, and this vision may seem to be inside your mind. The whitish glow that you see is the aura of your guardian angels.

Focus on that whitish glow, and breathe in and out deeply. Mentally say to your angels, *I would like to see you now.* You'll begin to see flashes of details of your angels. Keep looking above your shoulders. Don't focus directly on your own face, because it will seem to shift; and it may look like various other people during this exercise, which could greatly distract or even frighten you. Your face is merely doing this because you're tapping into your own self's "Akashic Records," or the "Book of Life." You are seeing visions of your soul's recorded history.

So, having angel visions during this exercise is contingent upon keeping your gaze above your head and around your shoulders.

Dream Work

You can mentally invite your deceased loved one, angel, or personal guide such as Jesus into your dreams at night. To have a powerful dream-time angel vision, you'll need to have a virtually drug-free day. This means to avoid, or just take in a minimum of, caffeine, sugar, chocolate, alcohol, nicotine, chamomile, melatonin, valerian, and other mood- or energy-altering substances. These drugs and herbs inhibit your REM sleep cycle, thus reducing and altering your dream patterns.

Before you go to sleep at night, write on a piece of paper to whomever you are inviting into your dream: "I would like to talk with you and see you. I ask that you enter my dreams tonight. I love you and deeply desire to see you." Then, put this paper under your pillow, and mentally repeat this request as you're falling asleep.

Most dream-time angel visions are extremely vivid. It is unlikely that you would forget a dream encounter with your angel or deceased loved one, especially if you go to sleep with a sober mind. However, it's always possible that your subconscious mind might cause you to forget having a dream if it knew that your waking mind couldn't handle this fact.

You may need to repeat this exercise for several days in a row before you actually have a dream-time angel vision. And you may find that after you've asked on successive days to see your angel, your big dream occurs on the night when you just let it go and surrender the whole thing to God.

Looking Sideways

After you meditate, mentally ask your angels or deceased loved one to appear to you. Then look out of the corner of your eye around the room. Some people have greater success seeing the spirit world peripherally, rather than looking straight ahead. It seems that when we look out of the side of our eye, we're more open to seeing things that our forward vision may block from our conscious awareness.

Asking for a Sign

Angel visions also include seeing "signs" in the physical world that are evidence of your angels' presence. You can mentally ask your angel or deceased loved one to send you a sign that will, for example, help you know which decision is best for you. You can also ask for a sign just to let you know that the being is with you.

Your task is to notice the sign as it is delivered. Fortunately, if you don't notice it at first, it will be repeated until you do. This repetition also helps dispel any skepticism you may have about the validity of the sign.

Common signs include seeing feathers, birds, butterflies, rainbows, and flowers. You could also see license plates, billboards, or paintings that have significance to you. In addition, some signs are auditory, such as when you repeatedly hear a song that was meaningful to you and your deceased loved one, or when you hear ringing in one ear.

In addition, your angels may help you see glowing or sparkling lights, as a sign that they are near. These "angel trails" are the electrical spark of the heavenly beings moving across space.

No matter how clearly or how fuzzy your angel vision, it's essential to mentally thank God and the angels for their help. When we are happy, peaceful, and grateful, that is heaven's reward for all of the assistance that they give us.

∾∾∾

Afterword

You already connect with your angels in many wonderful ways, including through the dreams, feelings, and signs you receive. Reading angel stories also tends to increase your awareness of the presence of angels in your life. So, just the process of reading this book will likely create an angel experience, of which you'll be consciously aware.

I find that our emotional climate can either breed or block angel connections. When we have an extremely strong emotion—such as fear, anger, or worry—and we simultaneously appeal to heaven for help, this often triggers an angel experience. However, if we have these strong emotions and *don't* ask for help, we can actually block ourselves from hearing their guidance. So, asking is the essential key.

You can request aid from God, Holy Spirit, Jesus (or other ascended masters), the archangels, your guardian angel, or a deceased loved one in so many different ways:

- **Think the thought:** *Help me!* Heaven hears our thoughts, and responds with assistance.

- **Speak your request aloud.** The words you choose, and the way that you say them, are unimportant. What counts is sincerity.

- **Write a letter to heaven.** Pour your heart out, including all your fears, worries, and hopes. Again, don't worry about being "proper." They're angels, not English teachers.

- **Invite them into your dreams.** Before falling asleep, pray to have a connection with your angels. Invite them (or a particular being in heaven) into your dreams. It's also helpful to write down your prayer and place the piece of paper under your pillow.

- **Ask for a sign.** Ask your angels to make their presence known through one of the ways discussed in the angel stories, and in the chapters in Part II. Don't specify how you want the sign to appear. Let the angels surprise you with their method. But *do* ask the angels to make it a very clear sign that you won't overlook.

- **Ask for faith.** If you find yourself filled with self-doubt, ask your angels to boost your spiritual confidence. Even if you're unsure whether you have angels, or whether they really exist, ask anyway. The easiest way is to mentally speak to your angels before falling asleep. Appeal to them to buoy your faith, and to connect with you so that you're sure of their presence.

You *are* surrounded by angels, right now. Even if you're a non-believer, you have guardian angels who love you, and who are with you, at this very moment. Close your eyes for a moment, breathe deeply, and feel their presence. If you still can't sense the angels, keep going. They're even more motivated to make their presence known than you are. They love you so much, and want to become more involved in your life.

Imagine for a moment what it must be like to be a guardian angel. Do you think it's a stressful or frustrating job? Our angels' purpose is to help bring peace upon Earth, one person at a time. When we ask for help, and allow them to help us, we're helping the angels fulfill their missions.

When my guardian angel saved my life during an armed carjacking in July of 1995, I learned a very important lesson: God could send angels to help save my life, but it was up to *me* to accept that help. A voice had warned me that my car would be stolen that day unless I put the top up on my convertible. I ignored this warning, and it almost cost me my life. Fortunately, during the carjacking, the angels gave me a second chance. They told me to scream with all my might! This time I listened!

My life was spared because I *allowed* God and the angels to help me. That moment changed me forever. I now know the importance of asking the angels for help, and then following their guidance when it comes. This may be one of the most important positive habits that anyone can develop.

Connecting with our angels, then, is much more than just a personal-growth venture. It's a relationship that helps us remember and work on our Divine life purpose, and to enact God's plan of peace. It's a relationship that could make a life-and-death difference for ourselves and our loved ones.

Our relationship with God, the ascended masters, our angels, and deceased loved ones can ultimately help us love ourselves and others more deeply. By opening our hearts to heaven, we literally open to life itself. In that way, we can all become earth angels.

— *Doreen*

About the Author

Doreen Virtue holds B.A., M.A., and Ph.D. degrees in counseling psychology; and is a lifelong clairvoyant who works with the angelic realm. She is the author of the *Healing with the Angels* book and oracle cards; *Archangels & Ascended Masters;* and *Angel Therapy®*, among other works. Her products are available in most languages worldwide.

Doreen has appeared on *Oprah,* CNN, *The View,* and other television and radio programs; and writes regular columns for *Woman's World, New Age Retailer,* and *Spirit & Destiny* magazines. For more information on Doreen and the workshops she presents, please visit: **www.AngelTherapy.com.**

You can listen to Doreen's live weekly radio show, and call her for a reading, by visiting **HayHouseRadio.com®.**

Notes

Notes

Notes

Notes

Notes

Notes

Notes

Notes

Notes

Notes

HAY HOUSE TITLES OF RELATED INTEREST

YOU CAN HEAL YOUR LIFE, the movie, starring Louise L. Hay & Friends
(available as a 1-DVD program and an expanded 2-DVD set)
Watch the trailer at: **www.LouiseHayMovie.com**

THE SHIFT, the movie,
starring Dr. Wayne W. Dyer
(available as a 1-DVD program and an expanded 2-DVD set)
Watch the trailer at: **www.DyerMovie.com**

ASK AND IT IS GIVEN: Learning to Manifest Your Desires,
by Esther and Jerry Hicks (The Teachings of Abraham®)

THE DIVINE NAME: The Sound That Can Change the World,
by Jonathan Goldman (book-with-CD)

*MODERN-DAY MIRACLES: Miraculous Moments and Extraordinary
Stories from People All Over the World Whose Lives Have Been Touched
by Louise L. Hay,* by Louise L. Hay & Friends

*THE POWER OF INTENTION: Learning to Co-create
Your World Your Way,* by Dr. Wayne W. Dyer

*THE TIMES OF OUR LIVES: Extraordinary True Stories of Synchronicity,
Destiny, Meaning, and Purpose,* by Louise L. Hay & Friends

*VISIONS, TRIPS, AND CROWDED ROOMS: Who and What You See
Before You Die,* by David Kessler

All of the above are available at your local bookstore,
or may be ordered by contacting Hay House (see next page).

We hope you enjoyed this Hay House book. If you'd like to receive our online catalog featuring additional information on Hay House books and products, or if you'd like to find out more about the Hay Foundation, please contact:

Hay House, Inc., P.O. Box 5100, Carlsbad, CA 92018-5100
(760) 431-7695 or (800) 654-5126
(760) 431-6948 (fax) or (800) 650-5115 (fax)
www.hayhouse.com® • **www.hayfoundation.org**

Published and distributed in Australia by: Hay House Australia Pty. Ltd., 18/36 Ralph St., Alexandria NSW 2015 • Phone: 612-9669-4299 • Fax: 612-9669-4144 • **www.hayhouse.com.au**

Published and distributed in the United Kingdom by: Hay House UK, Ltd., 292B Kensal Rd., London W10 5BE • Phone: 44-20-8962-1230 • Fax: 44-20-8962-1239 • **www.hayhouse.co.uk**

Published and distributed in the Republic of South Africa by: Hay House SA (Pty), Ltd., P.O. Box 990, Witkoppen 2068 • Phone/Fax: 27-11-467-8904 • **www.hayhouse.co.za**

Published in India by: Hay House Publishers India, Muskaan Complex, Plot No. 3, B-2, Vasant Kunj, New Delhi 110 070 • Phone: 91-11-4176-1620 • Fax: 91-11-4176-1630 • **www.hayhouse.co.in**

Distributed in Canada by: Raincoast, 9050 Shaughnessy St., Vancouver, B.C. V6P 6E5 • Phone: (604) 323-7100 • Fax: (604) 323-2600 • **www.raincoast.com**

Take Your Soul on a Vacation

Visit **www.HealYourLife.com®** to regroup, recharge, and reconnect with your own magnificence. Featuring blogs, mind-body-spirit news, and life-changing wisdom from Louise Hay and friends.

Visit **www.HealYourLife.com** today!

Don't miss the latest in books, CDs, movies, and events featuring best-selling author Doreen Virtue

**Angel Therapy®
Oracle Cards**
978-1-4019-1833-0
$15.95 USA · Card Deck

Solomon's Angels
978-1-4019-2324-2
$23.95 USA · 5-CD Set

**The Miracles of
Archangel Michael**
978-1-4019-2205-4
$19.95 USA · Hardcover

Available everywhere books are sold.

See Doreen in a city near you!
Visit **www.angeltherapy.com** for information on upcoming events and lectures.

hayhouseradio.com®

www.hayhouse.com®

HEAL YOUR LIFE♥
www.healyourlife.com®

Mind Your Body,
Mend Your Spirit

Hay House is the ultimate resource for inspirational and health-conscious books, audio programs, movies, events, e-newsletters, member communities, and much more.

Visit **www.hayhouse.com**® today and nourish your soul.

UPLIFTING EVENTS

Join your favorite authors at live events in a city near you or log on to **www.hayhouse.com** to visit with Hay House authors online during live, interactive Web events.

INSPIRATIONAL RADIO

Daily inspiration while you're at work or at home. Enjoy radio programs featuring your favorite authors, streaming live on the Internet 24/7 at **HayHouseRadio.com**®. Tune in and tune up your spirit!

VIP STATUS

Join the Hay House VIP membership program today and enjoy exclusive discounts on books, CDs, calendars, card decks, and more. You'll also receive 10% off all event reservations (excluding cruises). Visit **www.hayhouse.com/wisdom** to join the Hay House Wisdom Community™.

Visit **www.hayhouse.com** and enter priority code 2723
during checkout for special savings!
(One coupon per customer.)

HAY
HOUSE

HAYHOUSE
RADIO))
radio for your soul™

HAY HOUSE
Wisdom

Heal Your Life One Thought at a Time . . . on Louise's All-New Website!

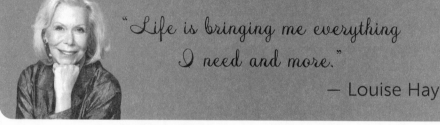

"Life is bringing me everything I need and more."

— Louise Hay

Come to HEALYOURLIFE.COM today and meet the world's best-selling self-help authors; the most popular leading intuitive, health, and success experts; up-and-coming inspirational writers; and new like-minded friends who will share their insights, experiences, personal stories, and wisdom so you can heal your life and the world around you . . . one thought at a time.

Here are just some of the things you'll get at HealYourLife.com:

- DAILY AFFIRMATIONS
- CAPTIVATING VIDEO CLIPS
- EXCLUSIVE BOOK REVIEWS
- AUTHOR BLOGS
- LIVE TWITTER AND FACEBOOK FEEDS
- BEHIND-THE-SCENES SCOOPS
- LIVE STREAMING RADIO
- "MY LIFE" COMMUNITY OF FRIENDS

PLUS:
FREE Monthly Contests and Polls
FREE BONUS gifts, discounts,
and newsletters

Make It Your Home Page Today!
www.HealYourLife.com®

HEAL YOUR LIFE ♥